ASSISI

the city of Saint Francis

art

history

spirituality

Editrice *tau*

The Canticle

Most High, all-powerful, good Lord,
Yours are the praises, the glory, the honour, and all blessing.
To You alone, Most High, do they belong, and no man is worthy to mention Your name.

Praised be You, my Lord, with all your creatures, especially Brother Sun,
Who is the day and through whom you give us light.

And he is beautiful and radiant with great splendour,
and bears a likeness of You, Most High One.

Praised be You, my Lord, through Sister Moon and the stars, in heaven you formed them
clear and precious and beautiful.

Praised be You, my Lord, through Brother Wind, and through the air, cloudy and serene,
and every kind of weather through which You give sustenance to Your creatures.

Praised be You, my Lord, through Sister Water, which is most useful
and humble and precious and chaste.

Praised be You, my Lord, through Brother Fire, through whom you light the night
and he is beautiful and playful and robust and strong,

Praised be You, my Lord, through Sister Mother Earth, who sustains us and governs us
and who produces varied fruits with coloured flowers and herbs.

Praised be You, my Lord, through those who give pardon for Your love,
and bear infirmity and tribulation.

Blessed are those who endure in peace for by You, Most High, they shall be crowned.

Praised be You, my Lord, through our Sister Bodily Death,
from whom no living man can escape.

Woe to those who die in mortal sin.
Blessed are those whom death will find in Your most holy will,
for the second death shall do them no harm.

Praise and bless my Lord, and give Him thanks and serve Him with great humility.
AMEN

History of the City

Assisi sits along the slopes of Mount Subasio enjoying an enviable view over the plain across which flow the Topino, Chiascio and Maroggia rivers. All around are the sub-Apennine hills of Perugia and the Martani Mountains.

It would seem that this area was first inhabited in the Neolithic era but it was not until the 6th century BC that the first Italic people, the Umbri, settled here. It was, however, not until the Hellenic period that a town in the architectural sense of an urban structure we know today was formed.

There are three legends surrounding the foundation of Assisi. The first legend would have Dardano, son of Electra, as the founder, the second has the brother of the Queen of Troy, Asio (who gave his name to Mount Subasio), as the founder. The third legend relates how Minerva founded Assisi after she fled from the attacks of Juno.

Under the Romans, Assisi was a *municipium* and the inhabitants were members of the Sergius tribe. Today, archaeological remains of the Roman era are still visible, including the portico of the Temple of Minerva with its six Corinthian columns supporting an elegant pediment, the Roman Forum, the Theatre and the Amphitheatre. The Monastery of St Quiricus is over the site of the former Temple dedicated to Mars. Assisi was also the birthplace of the Roman poet Sextus Aurelius Propertius (born in 46 BC) a member of an old Roman family: the *gens Propertia*. Others from Assisi were the poets Aulo Sabinio, Paolo Passeno and Sabina Vibia, wife of Emperor Hadrian.

The first bishop of the city was St Rufinus, former bishop of Amasia in Asia Minor, where both he and his son, Cesidio, following ferocious persecution had been imprisoned. When they were freed they came to Italy staying first in Abruzzo before moving to Assisi. However, only Rufinus reached Assisi as Cesidio had suffered martyrdom, along with his companions between 235 and 238 AD. Rufinus himself was also courageous and preached the Gospel until he too was thrown into prison where he was terribly tortured: his cheeks were battered with stones, he was whipped and if that were not enough he was put in an oven to be burned alive but the flames went out. He was finally drowned by having boulders tied around his neck. His body was recovered and, following a series of vicissitudes, is now in the crypt of the cathedral dedicated to him.

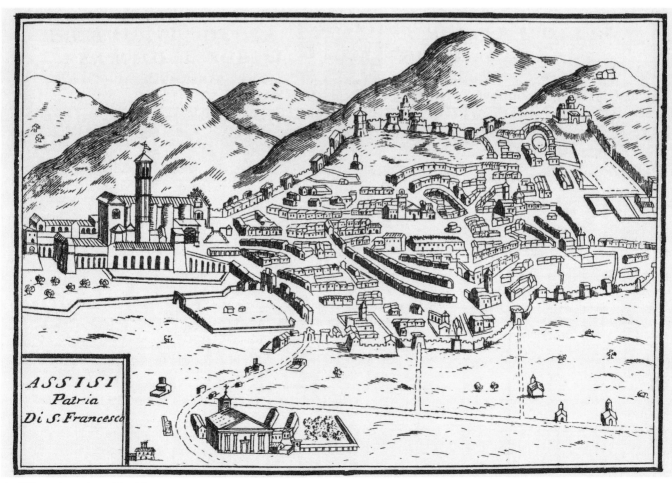

An 18th century view of Assisi.

Nepis and Fiumi

The two most important families who held power in Assisi from the medieval period were the Nepis and Fiumi. The Nepis, head of the Parte di Sopra, arrived in Assisi, according to tradtion, in 767 with Duke Teutone. They held the ancient feud of Bandita between Assisi and Nocera. Francesco Nepis was a knight of Malta in 1379, and Carlo Nepis was Bishop of Assisi in 1456. The Fiumi, head of a faction of the Parte di Sopra, counted among their ancestors Ortolana Fiumi, St Clare's mother. Others of note were Guido Fiumi, podestà (mayor) of Orvieto in 1309, Jacopo, abbot of St Peter's Monastery in 1429, and Ulderico, a poet and man of letters in the 17th century. In 1462 the family was invested with the lordship of the Castle of Sterpeto.

Upper Church. Giotto's *Francis before Honorius III* (detail).

During the barbarian invasions and the Ostrogothic War (535-553) Assisi was victim to a series of devastations and sackings caused by Totila's Ostrogothic Army until the town fell under the dominium of the powerful Lombard Duchy of Spoleto. In the Medieval period Frederick Barbarossa entrusted the city to his vassal, Conrad of Lutzen, Duke of Spoleto, who built, as a symbol of Imperial power, the Great Fortress (the Rocca Maggiore) overlooking the city. According to tradition, Barbarossa's grandson, Frederick the Great of Swabia, was born in Assisi.

With the birth of the Commune, Assisi achieved complete independence becoming one of the most powerful Umbrian towns. In this period Assisi was repeatedly in conflict with nearby rival Perugia. In 1237, Assisi's autonomy was confirmed when Pope Gregory IX granted Assisi the right to nominate its own officers including the podestà (or mayor).

Assisi began a slow but thorough reconstruction under Cardinal Egidio Albornoz, who played a key role in Assisi's breaking free from Perugia.

Autonomy was to be short-lived as the great lords of the time imposed their hegemony on the town. In 1400 Assisi submitted to Gian Galeazzo Visconti only to fall, at Visconti's death, into internal conflict caused by the two most powerful families: the Nepis and the Fiumi. Order was restored by the Perugian *condottiere*, Braccio da Montone, in 1419. Braccio was succeeded by Francesco Sforza, under whose dominion the town came under the control of the Papal States.

St Francis and Franciscanism

Thus did the Lord give unto me Brother Francis to start his penitence. When I was a sinner it was too bitter a thing to look on lepers. But the Lord Himself took me among them and I was merciful with them. When I left them, what was bitter was turned into a sweetness of the soul and body, I stayed awhile and then left earthly things." These words are from the first lines of the testament of St Francis and allow us to see the sense of total dedication to God and the outcasts which was to be the road the Saint and his companions were to take. Complete poverty which permitted the total spiritual, mystic experience of giving oneself to others, thus following the

4

teachings of the Gospel in the best way possible.

The story of Francis starts in the winter of 1182 when he was born to the wealthy cloth merchant Pietro Bernardone and Lady Pica. Nothing is known of him until 1202 when he participated in the war against Perugia in the Battle of Collestrada when he was captured. In 1205 he was, as a knight, heading for the South of Italy in order to join the crusade of Walter of Brienne. However, at Spoleto Francis had a vision that he "should have been serving the Master rather than the servant" (that is God and not Walter of Brienne) and so he headed back at once to Assisi and started dedicating himself to an ascetic life, one of privation and sacrifice. He went among the outcasts giving them the money he had previously wasted on entertainment and began to care for the lepers who lived in isolation outside the city walls.

One day Francis came upon the country church of San Damiano, and there, while in prayer before the Crucifix he heard the following words: "Go, Francis, and repair my house, you see falling into ruin". He did not at first understand the general or spiritual meaning of the words but took them literally and restored not only the church of San Damiano but also that of the Porziuncola at Santa Maria degli Angeli.

Through a profound reading of the Gospel St Francis came to understand that the Disciples of Christ should not have any worldly possessions, no money, no clothes, no shoes or any other clothing, so Francis stripped himself of all his clothes save a rough tunic. In a short time, he was joined by his first followers and with them he began the difficult path to a purification of the soul under the protection of the incumbent of the See of Assisi, Bishop Guido who took an interest in the new group of reformers.

Lower Church, Right Transept. *St Francis* by Cimabue.

In the little church of the Porziuncola St Francis and his disciples, alternated moments of prayer with untiring assistance to the poor and to lepers, thus offering the inhabitants of the area an example of a true Christian life and charity. Between 1209 and 1210 the "brethren" came before Pope Innocent III who approved their Rule which was set out in a few, but profound, precepts. In 1221, there was a further, unofficial, Rule, known as the *non bullata*, based on vows of obedience, chasti-

Lower Church. *Sermon to the Birds* by the Master of St Francis.

ty, and, obviously, complete poverty. However, as the Pope did not entirely agree with the harshness such a life imposed a successive, less strict Rule called the *bullata* was drawn up in 1223 and was immediately confirmed by Pope Honorius III.

The teachings of St Francis were now a model to be imitated, an example to follow for the whole Church for in St Francis could be found those instances of poverty and purity which had for so long been put aside. Throughout his life St Francis renounced everything material and earthly including ordination as a priest so that he could remain a one of the Friars Minor, thus underlining his humbleness.

There are so many episodes con-cerning the life of St Francis, among which the following three deserve to be mentioned. One night St Francis was taken by an irresistible carnal longing to abate which he tried to abate with flagellation, but with little success, he then came out of his cell and began to roll in the snow and then built seven snowmen and then talking to his flesh, said "behold, the largest is your wife, of these four, two are sons and two are daughters, the others are your manservant and your maid for your service.

Go make haste and clothe them all for they are freezing to death. Should this be too much for, serve diligently none but the Lord". After these words the devil in him left in a much confused state and Francis could then, with his soul at peace, return to his cell.

The second episode refers to the wolf of Gubbio. This huge fierce beast had appeared in the city and had begun to devour not only animals but also humans, creating much havoc. Francis then decided to meet this terrible creature and after having blessed the animal said "come hither Brother Wolf, I command you in the name of Christ to do no harm to either me or any other man". The wolf then fell at the Saint's feet and became as meek as a lamb. Seeing the change in the wolf, Francis said: "Brother Wolf, as long as you keep this peace and live among men I will make sure that you need never hunger again. In exchange for this I

6

want you, Brother Wolf, to promise that you will harm neither man nor animal. Do you promise?" The wolf then bowed its head as a sign that he promised what St Francis asked.

Another episode reveals further side to St Francis's personality: that of the fun lover. The 8th of May 1213 during the Feast of the Apparition of the Archangel St Michael on the Gargano Peninsula, Francis reached the square of St Leo in Montefeltro full of people celebrating the dubbing of a knight. At the high point of the Feast St Francis leapt up onto a low wall and repeated a love song that had just been sung by a jester: "So much is the goodness I await that I can endure every pain". Francis then reinterpreted the words in a Christian sense explaining that such is the goodness that comes from divine love that any type of pain is of little consequence.

A noble lord, Orlando of Chiusi, was so impressed by St Francis that he granted him the mountain of La Verna. It was here that on the morning of 17th September that Francis received the stigmata on his hands and feet. Coming down from the mount, in pain for the various ailments from which he suffered, he began a period of slow agony. Among the words, which had opened the hearts of thousands of the faithful, are: "Fear and holy simplicity confound all worldly wisdom and knowledge of the flesh. Holy poverty confounds greed and avarice and the worries of this world. Holy humility confounds pride and all men and all things of this world. Holy charity confounds all diabolical and worldly temptation and all human fears."

After his last sermons at the start of 1225, the increasingly tired and ill Francis retired to the Convent of San Damiano and it was here that he composed the *Cantico delle Creature*. His health was worsening so much that St Francis said he was about to join "Sister Death". St Fran-

cis left his earthly life 3rd October 1226, naked in the ashes and comforted by his brothers. He was Canonized by Pope Gregory IX 16 July 1228 leaving the members of his three orders an example of a wondrous religious experience.

In 1230 Gregory IX modified the Rule of the Order so that while the Franciscans could not themselves have possessions they were authorized to benefit from donations or legacies. This caused splits within

the Order with on one side the so-called Spirituals, who held that were the true followers of the true Franciscan Rule, and the other side were the so-called Conventuals who were more inclined to accept the Pope's reforms.

The Spirituals were to have but a short life and by the 14th century their protests at the changes were no longer heard. However, the divergences concerning the Franciscan Rule continued as there was a further

Lower Church. Detail of the St John the Baptist Chapel by Pietro Lorenzetti.

split in the group known as the Observers who were faithful to the principles of austerity, which had been upheld by the Spirituals, and the Conventuals, who were more for a less strict Rule which was more in keeping with the times. Pope Leo X's papal bull of 1517 established a subdivision of the Order into the Minors and the Conventual Minors. Among the members of the former was Clare who had entered the church of San Damiano with other sisters, thus forming the Second Franciscan Order, the female branch later known as the "Poor Clares".

A third Franciscan Order, the Capuchins, was sanctioned by Pope Clement VII in 1528. At that time the Catholic world, and the Holy See in particular, found itself having to face the Protestant reform and therefore felt the need to favour those religious groups which based themselves on the true values of the Gospel. Thus, the Order of Capuchins, or the *fratres minores*, as the Order was at first known, was founded. The Order was founded in the Marches by Matthew of Bascio and, in 1529, it passed under the guide of Ludovico of Fossombrone. The Order enjoyed popularity at once thanks to its dynamism and exemplary role among the faithful. Along with the spread of the Franciscan Order was that of the Order of Penitents, better known as the Third Order, which accepted lay members of whom no vows were required. Members of the "Tertiaries" included Margherita da Cortona (1247-1297) and Angela da Foligno (1248-1309).

The three male Franciscan Orders were recognisable by the colour of their habits: the Conventuals wore black with a white cord, the Minors wore brown with a white cord, while the Capuchins had a similar habit to that of the Minors but with a longer more pointed hood.

Rufinus

Rufinus is mentioned in the first of the passages of St Francis as being among the first 12 of the Saint's companions. However, not all sources agree, as it would seem that Rufinus was not in fact among the first group of companions. What is however recalled is "Rufinus' virtuous relentless praying, even when asleep and whatever he would do he would always do with his spirit with the Lord". Rufinus probably had a stutter and was told by St Francis to go and pray naked. In Verse XXXI Francis described Rufinus as "one of the three most holy souls in the world". Rufinus nursed Francis during his illness and once touched the wound in Francis' side. Rufinus is buried near the tomb of St Francis in the Basilica of Assisi.

Below: View of Assisi from Santa Maria degli Angeli.

Opposite above: The Upper Church.

The Patriarchal Basilica of St Francis

Following the death of St Francis, in 1226, his successor Brother Elias received some land on the slopes of Mount Subasio in an area called the "Colle dell'Inferno" (the Hill of Hell), and 17th July 1228 Pope Gregory IX laid the first stone for the erection of the Basilica.

Work on the Basilica progressed rapidly and after just two years the body of St Francis was transferred to the Basilica where to this day the Saint is venerated.

At the same time as the Basilica was going up, the Convent was also being built to a plan based on that symbol so dear to St Francis, the Tau. The building consists of the Lower Church, which also functions as a crypt where the body of the Saint lies and appears somewhat squashed and poorly illuminated, a sort of grotto which, because of its extraordinary iconography, inspires meditation, prayer, reflection and a peaceful veneration of the Saint. From here, the visitor

passes to the Upper Church, which contrary to the Lower Church place, offers luminosity in a single nave which, after having followed the well-defined spiritual path of the Saint's life projects the pilgrims' faith upwards to Heaven and the love of God.

The Basilica is reached through the 14th century door of St Francis. After then turning left along the road dedicated to Brother Elias is **Piazza Inferiore** surrounded by low arcades which give the visitor the idea of being in the cloisters of a convent. To the left, at the top, is the 13th century portal of the Oratory of St Bernardino of Siena in front of the entrance to the Convent and on the right the door leading to the Lower Church.

The Lower Church.

The Lower Church

The portal is in marble with two mullioned windows over which can be admired a central rose window accompanied by two smaller ones, the whole being protected by a large prothyrum. Inside, on the left, is the **Chapel of St Sebastian** which has frescoes by the Assisi artists Girolamo Martelli (1645) and Cesare Sermei. On the right, on the elegant gothic mausoleum of Giovanni dè Cerchi, is a curious porphyry vase which was traditionally sent by the Queen of Cyprus to hold the paint. Then, after the Tribune commissioned in 1458 by the noble Nepis family, is another funeral monument which holds the mortal remains of John of Brienne. At the end of the right side wall is the Chapel dedicated to St Anthony the Abbot, erected in 1360, with a series of frescos of the history of the saint by Cesare Sermei (1581-1668) and Girolamo Martelli in 1610. From here, one comes to the

Lower Church. Detail of St Catherine's Chapel, Cardinal Egidio Albornoz kneeling.

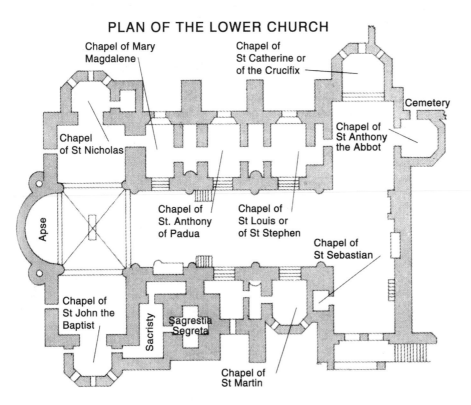

PLAN OF THE LOWER CHURCH

Chapel of Mary Magdalene

Chapel of St Catherine or of the Crucifix

Cemetery

Chapel of St Anthony the Abbot

Chapel of St Nicholas

Chapel of St. Anthony of Padua

Chapel of St Louis or of St Stephen

Chapel of St Sebastian

Apse

Chapel of St John the Baptist

Sacristy

Sagrestia Segreta

Chapel of St Martin

Plan of the Lower Chrurch.

Lower Church. Detail of the right side.

suggestive cemetery. Returning back, on the right is the **Chapel of Saint Catherine**, commissioned by Cardinale Egidio Albornoz in 1367. There are 18 figures of saints together with eight histories of the Saint's life frescoed by Andrea dè Bartoli from Bologna, in 1368: *The Arrest of Saint Catherine, Saint Catherine Before the Emperor Maximum, St Francis Converses with the Infant Jesus, Disputing with the Doctors, the Conversion of the Empress Faustina, Martyrdom of the Empress, Martyrdom of the Saint* and, the last scene, *The Executioner's Punishment*. The nave is a wide dark hall with large rib vaults.

The vast pictorial cycle, as with the Upper Church, did not serve a purely decorative purpose but is a symbolic instrument that was also a sort theological treatise centred on the themes of Poverty and the life of the Saint.

Along the walls of the nave are the frescos of the "Master of St Francis", carried out in around 1253. On the right wall from the first bay fresco fragments show *Ecce mater tua*, *the Death of Christ, the Descent from the Cross, the Deposition from the Cross* and the *Deposition in the Sepulchre*. On the left wall, looking towards the altar, it is possible to admire the first iconographical representations of the histories of St Francis: *The Renunciation of Worldly Goods, The Dream of Innocent III, The Saint Speaking to the Birds, Receiving the Stigmata* and *The Saint's Death*.

The first chapel on the right,

Right: Lower Church, right transept, *Crucifixion* (Giotto).

Following page: Lower Church, right transept, *Madonna and Child and St Francis* (Cimabue).

Lower Church. View of the vaults and the left transept.

commissioned by Cardinal Gentile of Montefiore, is dedicated to **St Louis**. The chapel is rectangular and the lower part is decorated in red and white marble, while the frescoes above showing the life of St Stephen are by Dono Doni (1575). In the panels between the vault ribs are the Prophets and the four Sibyls.

The second chapel, to **St Anthony of Padua** (who joined the Franciscan Order at Pentacost 1221 at the Porziuncola), was frescoed by Cesare Sermei and Girolamo Martelli (1610) with scenes from the Saint's life.

Next comes the **Chapel of Mary Magdalene**, another Saint consecrated to the poor and an example of that holiness all sinful people can strive towards. The chapel, entirely by Giotto and his pupils, has a square plan with a cross vault with light from a large clerestory window. The wall decorations show episodes of the life of Mary Magdalene: *Christ and Mary Magdalene in the Parsee's House, The Resurrection of Lazarus, Mary Magdalene receiving Communion from St Massimino, the Noli me tangere, Mary Magdalene Landing at Marseille* and the *Saint with the Angels*.

In the lunette above the entrance is the *Hermit Zosimo Giving his Cloak to Mary Magdalene*.

The right hand side is also covered by precious frescos. The vault has episodes of the life of the Our Lady and of Jesus, by Giotto's pupil, Taddeo Gaddi: *The Visitation to Saint Elisabeth, The Birth of Jesus, The Adoration of the Magi, The Presentation at the Temple, Flight into Egypt, The Slaughter of the Innocent, Jesus Disputing with the Doctors, The Return to Nazareth*. On the right wall is a striking *Crucifixion* attributed to Giotto and, next to this, Cimabue's famous masterpiece the *Madonna Enthroned with the Child, St Francis and four Angels*.

Over the entrance of the **St Nicholas Chapel** is a painting of the *Annunciation*, lower down is the *Miraculous Recovery of the Little Boy of Sessa*, this work is divided by the arch into two episodes, on the left, *The Boy's Death under the Rubble* and, on the right, *Resurrection for the Intervention of Francis*.

Along the right wall are paintings by Simone Martini (1285-1344) and his brother, Donato, of *St Francis*, *St Ludovic*, *St Elisabeth*, *the Blessed Delfina*, *St Elzearius*. Further on, there is a *Madonna and Child* and *St Elisabeth and St Louis*. Moving on, under the fresco by Cimabue, are paintings of the *Blessed Giovanni Inglese* and the *Blessed Bernard da Quintavalle*, *Sylvester*, *William*, *Eletto* and *Valentine*.

The chapel at the short right end of the transept is dedicated to **St Nicholas of Bari**, another Saint who devoted his whole life to helping orphans, widows and the poor. Cardinal Gian Gaetano Orsini, whose sepulchre is in the end wall, had the chapel was erected in 1310. The chapel has frescoes by Giotto's pupils dating from the early 14th century showing 12 saints and scenes of the life of St Nicholas by Palmerino di Guido: *St Nicolas Resuscitating a Boy from the Flames, Freeing a Believer from Slavery, an Enslaved Son Returned to his Parents, St Nicholas beaten by order of the Emperor Licinius, the Saint giving a Dowry to Three Poor Girls, Election to Bishop of Mira, Episcopal Consecration, Three convicts freed from death, Shipwreck saved by the Saint, the Apparition to the Emperor Constantine.*

The Cosmatesque Main Altar, consecrated in 1253, is in the presbytery. In the confession below is the tomb of St Francis. The chancel of 1471 is by Apollonio of Ripatransone and the apse was frescoed with the *Universal Judgment* by Caesar Sermei in 1623.

In the vault panels above, there are the four famous frescoes traditionally attributed to Giotto. These represent the allegories of Franciscan virtues, a synthesis of the Franciscan Rule with the allegorical representations of the Holiness St

Lower Church. *Allegory of Chastity.*

Lower Church. *Allegory of Poverty.*

Lower Church. *Allegory of Obedience.*

Lower Church. *Glory of St Francis.*

Francis reached by observing three vows, rather than the three capital vices: Obedience not Pride; Poverty not Avarice; Chastity not Lust.

Chastity is symbolised as a castle on a hill, surrounded by a wall and turrets. In the first circle of the walls are two heavenly virtues with hexagonal haloes, to whom is entrusted the internal defence of chastity: Saint Purity (*munditia*) and Saint Fortitude (*fortitudo*). The outer defence of the castle rests with the elders with their wisdom and shields and clubs ready to withstand external attacks.

Outside the walls, a young knight is being bathed in holy water, the symbol of spiritual rebirth, he then receives the white ensign which Purity hands to him from the wall while Fortitude gives him a shield to protect himself. On the left St Francis and Saint Clare welcome three pilgrims, and behind them winged Penitence fights carnal love off, shown as a boy with the feet of a harpy, with a lance.

Poverty is symbolised as an attractive, but poorly dressed, woman who is united in a mystical marriage with St Francis. Jesus himself blesses the wedding in the presence of holy personages surrounded by a ring of protecting angels. The bride is passing the ring to Hope, dressed in green. **Charity**, dressed in red and crowned with roses with three flames, offers the newlyweds her burning heart. The meaning of this is that poverty alone is sterile if it is not accompanied by Hope, Charity and Faith in Christ.

Above are two angels taking the symbols of terrestrial wealth which St Francis had renounced to Our Lord.

Obedience is portrayed as a winged figure sitting under an open loggia on the summit of one of the hills. This is virtue which is opposed to all the vices and thus im-

Lower Church. View of the vaults and the right transept.

poses her silence by putting a finger to her lips and placing the yoke of obedience upon the shoulders of a friar.

Assisting the ceremony are Prudence and Humility, the former with a double face of a young girl and that of an old woman as it considers both past and present things, causes and effects, and holds in hand a compass to measure words, a mirror for reflection and an astrolabe to conform its actions to universal harmony, the latter represented as a beautiful young girl holding

up a candle, the symbol of the divine light that has guided her. On top of the loggia is St Francis, the founder of the new Order, supported by the hands of the Lord reaching out to show that Obedience places men under the direct guidance of God.

Above the altar the **Triumph of St Francis** is idealized. The Saint, who appeared as a simple character in other allegories, no longer appears in a sackcloth habit but with a rich dalmatic, sat upon a throne and crowned by rejoicing angels.

The left arm, looking at the altar, was decorated between 1315 and 1320 by the Sienese master Pietro Lorenzetti (1280-1348) and his assistants.

There are scenes from the life of Christ which serve to reflect the scenes of the life of Francis in the right side, to confirm the similarity of the life of the Saint with that example of the Son of God and to confirm the saint as an *alter Cristus*.

Scenes of the life of Jesus, attributed to Pietro Lorenzetti, are de-

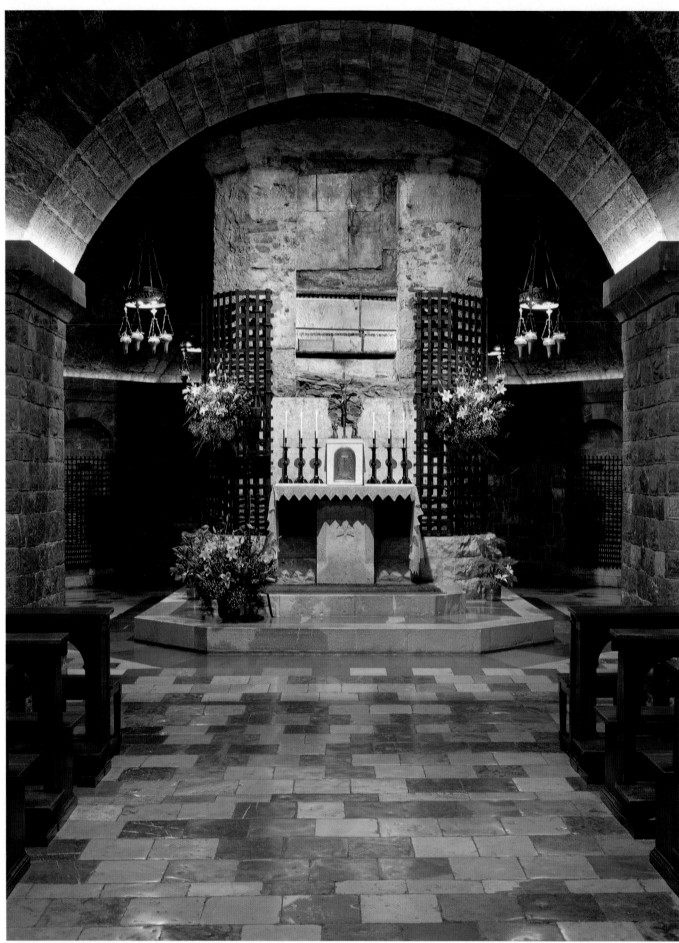

The Tomb of St Francis.

Lower Church. Left transept. St John the Baptist Chapel, *Madonna with Child, St John* and *St Francis* (Pietro Lorenzetti).

Simone Martini

Simone Martini (born in Siena in around 1284, died at Avignon in 1344) was influenced by the local (Duccio Buoninsegna) and the Florentine (Giotto) artistic tradition. Other influences came from Giovanni Pisano, the first of the great Italian sculptors, and from what he saw of refined Gothic objects from France (ivory and enamel). Martini's subjects, even the religious ones, had an aristocratic and knightly feel to them, differing from the historic and human accuracy of Giotto, as can be seen in the Palazzo Pubblico in Siena. His paintings are very intense, for instance, *St Louis of Toulouse Crowning Robert of Anjou* (Naples, Capodimonte Gallery) and the *Annunciation* in the Uffizi. In 1339 Simone Martini moved to the Papal Court at Avignon where his work (unfortunately, all lost) had a great influence on the development of international and French late Gothic art. While at Avignon, Martini met Petrarch for whom he illuminated the frontespiece of a codex by Virgil and painted the portrait of Laura (also lost).

Lower Church. Detail of St Martin's Chapel (Simone Martini).

Lower Church. Left transept. *Crucifixion* (Pietro Lorenzetti)

picted on the vaults: *Christ Enters Jerusalem, The Last Supper, Washing the Disciples Feet, Christ Betrayed, Judah hangs Himself, The Scourging, Towards Calvary, Deposition, The Tomb, Christ's Descent to Limbo, The Resurrection.* Here, on the left, is the marvellous *Crucifixion* by Lorenzetti, the most representative work of the cycle for its execution and use of colour, defined as one of the finest expressions of the dramatic genius of the Italian *trecento*. Below is the *Madonna and Child between St Francis and St John the Evangelist,* also known as the *Lady of the Sunsets,* which, because of its position,

is illuminated every day by the last light of the setting sun.

At the end is the **Chapel of St John the Evangelist**, erected in around 1310, where the *Madonna with Child and Saints Francis and John the Baptist* by Pietro Lorenzetti can be admired.

Moving back into the nave, the first chapel on the left is dedicated to **St Martin**, another saint devoted to protecting the poor who exhorted the rich to share their wealth with the needy.

The chapel was commissioned by Cardinal Gentile da Montefiore, a Franciscan, and frescoed by the Sienese painter Simone Martini be-

Lower Church, Tribune of St Stanislaw (detail)

22

Plan of the Upper Church.

NEW TESTAMENT

Jesus Christ, the New Adam	Passion of Christ	New Creature Imitatio Christi
Annunciation	Wedding of Cana	Liberation of the Penitent Heretic
		Confession of the Woman Raised from the Dead
Visitation (destroyed)	Lazarus Raised from the Dead (destroyed)	Francis Heals a Devotee
Nativity	Judah	Apparition to Gregory IX
		Francis is Canonised
Adoration of the Magi	Jesus Condemned (destroyed)	St Clare Mourns St Francis
Presentation at the Temple	Calvary	Jerome and the Stigmata
		Vision of the Brother Augustine and the Bishop of Assisi
Flight into Egypt	Death of Christ on the Cross	Death of St Francis
Jesus Teaching in the Temple	Christ Entombed	St Francis Receives the Stigmata on Mt Verna
		St Francis Appears at the Chapter of Arles
Baptism of Jesus in the River Jordan	The Three Marys at the Sepulchre	St Francis Preaches before Honorius III
		Death of the Knight of Celano

OLD TESTAMENT

New Creature Imitatio Christi	Old Testament Figures	The Creation and the Sin of Adamo
Homage of a Simple Man	Noah Builds the Ark	Creation
St Francis Gives his Cloak to a Poor Man		
Vision of the Palace Full of Arms	Noah Enters the Ark	Creation of Adamo
Miracle of the Crucifix at San Damiano	Abraham and the Sacrifice of Isaac	Creation of Eve
Renunciation of Wordly Goods		
Dream of Innocent III.	The Angels Come to Abraham	The Original Sin
Honorius III Approves the Rule of St Francis	Isaac Blesses Jacob	Expulsion from the Garden of Eden
Vision of St Francis and the Flaming Chariot		
Vision of Thrones	Esau and Isaac	The Trials of Adam and Eve
The Demons Cast Out of Arezzo	Joseph in the Well	The Sacrifice of Cain and Abel (destroyed)
St Francis before the Sultan		
Christ, the Source of His Activity	Joseph Forgives His Brothers	Cain Kills Abel
The Feast of the Incarnation		

Pietro Lorenzetti (1280-1348)

His first recorded work is the polyptych in the Pieve di Arezzo commissioned in 1320. In 1335, along with his brother, Ambrogio, he produced the frescoes (now lost) of the Hospital of Santa Maria della Scala.

Among the documented works (also lost) is the painting (1337) for the Church of San Martino in Siena.

In the early years of his activity Lorenzetti drew heavily on the work of Duccio di Buoninsegna, Giotto and Giovanni Pisano. His work includes such masterpieces as the Nativity of the Virgin (Museo dell'Opera, Siena), the altarpiece of Blessed Humility and the Madonna Enthroned with Child and Angels (Uffizi, Florence).

tween 1322 and 1326. The chapel has a rectangular plan with a barrel vault with an apse with three mullioned windows enriched with splendid stained glass.

Lower down, on the left, are the images of *St Francis, St Anthony, Mary Magdalene, Saints Catherine, Clare and Elizabeth*, the rest of the decoration, also by Martini, shows scenes from the life of St Martin: *Division of the Cloak; The Dream of St Martin; the Emperor Constance knights the Saint; St Martin ready to face the enemy; the Saint one of the Clergy; the Saint a Friar in* **Alberga** *preaching at Chartres, At the funeral of St* **Liborio**.

The next chapel is dedicated to **St Peter of Alcantara**. The window shows the *Apostle St Simon*. Then, the late 13th century apse richly decorated with polychrome marble and twisted columns.

Halfway along the nave is the entrance to the crypt where the body of St Francis lies together with the Blessed Brothers Rufinus, Masseo, Angelo and the Blessed Jacopa dei Settesoldi.

The body of St Francis is in the stone sarcophagus within the pilaster. Francis was laid to rest here by Brother Elias in 1230. It was not until 1818, after 52 days of work, that the others from the Sacred Convent could join Francis. The crypt was inaugurated in 1820 and has had its present form only since 1932.

The Lower Church is in itself an artistic treasure of rare beauty, a singular anthology of *trecento* art by two masters, Simone Martini and Pietro Lorenzetti. Siena, the birthplace of the two painters, was then the most representative centre from which the Gothic style spread. It was artists from the School of Siena who conceived one of the most ambitious artistic projects of the age in Assisi.

The Upper Church

On going back into the Upper Church through the small door set in the right transept, the visitor immediately perceives the difference between Upper and Lower Churches.

The Upper Church is spacious and bright and seems to reach out towards the heavens in a hymn of glory to the Lord, in a sort of spiritual resurrection.

The fresco cycle of the Upper Church is much more unitary, it is a marvellous construction based on religious doctrine and on sacred art. All the decorations express in a rigorous manner the unity and the finalities of the Church while keeping to an iconographic programme which is an incomparable teaching tool, a painted text.

The paintings form the pages of an open book so that the people could learn from the walls what they could not do from books. It is thus a work of great beauty, but not of mere aestheticism, with completely didactic purposes. The visit begins from the left transept, facing the altar, where that pictorial genius Cimabue worked between 1278 and 1285.

Here the "Celestial Jerusalem" is represented through the symbolic visions of the Apocalypse of St John the Evangelist aimed at strengthening Christian Faith with the certainty that the Church will exist until the end of time. Above is, the *Archangel Michael, Head of the Celestial Host* conquering evil represented by a dragon.

Lower down: *The Adoration of the Lamb on the Throne by twenty-four priests* surrounded by a choir of Angels to symbolize the believers who adore the innocent sacrificial victim; *The Vision of the four Angels* whose mission is to sepa-

Upper Church, left transept.

rate the believers from the enemies of the Lord; *The Vision of the Final Judgment* with the Angels heralding the advent of divine justice for which the world searches in vain; *The Vision of the Destruction of Babylon* to show the final, definitive defeat of evil; *St John on the Island of Patmos* being abducted by an Angel of the Lord and has a prophetic vision.

On the left wall is Cimabue's

Cenni di Peppi better known as Cimabue (1240/50 - 1302 ca)

Little is known of Cimabue's life until 1272. Cimabue worked in and remained faithful to the Byzantine manner but his expressiveness and innovations with colour opened the way for Giotto and the new Italian art. The second reference point for Cimabue is the Basilica of St Francis at Assisi, where he worked from around 1278 with the Sienese Duccio di Buoninsegna and the Florentine Giotto. Before Assisi, one of his most noteworthy works was the Crucifix in Santa Croce (1272c) with the body full of a new sensitiveness.

At the Uffizi in Florence, there is another of his masterpieces: the Madonna of the Santa Trinità. His only certain work (1301-1302) is a St John, part of the large mosaic in the apse of Pisa Cathedral.

Cimabue was considered a pupil of Giunta Pisano (first half of the 13th century) and in those years followed in the wake of Coppo di Marcovaldo and was later influenced by the Roman Pietro Cavallini.

Upper Church, left transept. *Apocalypse* (Cimabue).

Upper Church, left transept. *Crucifixion* (Cimabue).

Crucifixion to show how Jesus sacrificed himself for us to overcome sin and, at the same time, the Church and the faithful have to accept the Cross of Jesus to defeat evil.

At the foot of the cross is St Francis, again the *alter Cristus*, with his stigmata. The fresco, due to the lead oxide, a component in the colour, is completely blackened, this however, does not detract from considering the *Crucifixion* as one of the most tragic representations of the Passion of Christ.

The frescos on the right arm of the crossing, facing the altar, develop the theme of the Terrestrial Church with scenes of the lives of Saints Peter and Paul begun by the Master of St Francis and then continued by Cimabue.

The histories, in a clockwise direction from the gallery, are, *St Peter Heals the Cripple, St Peter Heals the Sick and Frees the Possessed, The Fall of Simon Magus, the Martyrdom of St Peter, the Martyrdom of St Paul.*

The powers Christ granted to His Apostles and how His followers had to be willing to make any sacrifice, even death, can be seen in the choice of the episodes here. There is another *Crucifixion* by Cimabue which also clearly underlines the final sacrifice as the culminating factor of Redemption. Between the Heavenly and Terrestrial Churches is the intermediary figure of the Virgin Mary to whom is reserved the central part of the choir.

The frescos, after an initial phase by the Master of St Francis, are the work of Cimabue: *Annunciation to Joachim, Joachim's Offer to the Temple, Nativity of the Virgin,* and the *Marriage of the Virgin.* Under the left gallery: *Mary Takes Leave of the Apostles, Death of the*

Upper Church, right transept. *Crucifixion* (Cimabue).

Upper Church, *Assumption of the Virgin.*

26

Upper Church. First bay. The restored vaults.

Giotto (1266-1337)

Giotto (Agnolo di Bordone) was, according to tradition, born around 1266 at Vespignano nel Mugello and received his early training in the bottega of Cimabue in the years 1282 and 1287.

Between 1290 and 1304 he frescoed the Upper Church in the Basilica of St Francis in Assisi and in the same period he also went to Rome for the first time. Between 1298 and 1303 his output was very intense and he travelled widely. After completing the fresco cycle at Assisi he began the decorations of the Chapel of St Nicholas in the Lower Church.

In 1300, during the first Jubilee called by Pope Boniface VIII, Giotto was in Rome where he probably designed the the Navicella, the large mosaic of the Ship of the Church. Giotto then moved on to Rimini and later to Padua where he stayed until 1305 as he was commissioned by Enrico Scrovegni to decorate the Arena Chapel. Between 1305 and 1310 he was in Florence

where he produced the Crucifix in the Church of San Felice in Piazza and the famous Ognisanti Madonna (Florence, Uffizi). From 1310 until 1313 he probably carried out the decorations in the Peruzzi Chapel in Santa Croce in Florence.

Critics agree that the vault panels of the right arm of the transept of the Lower Church in the Basilica of St Francis were decorated from 1315 to 1320 to his designs, with much work being done by his shop.

In October 1320 Giotto was once more in Florence when he produced the Stefaneschi Altar (now in the Vatican) and the frescoes of the Bardi Chapel in Santa Croce.

His presence in Florence is corroborated by various documents up to 1326 when, according to some sources, he began the Baroncelli Polyptych in Santa Croce.

On the 12th of April 1334 the local authorities of Florence nominated Giotto Master Mason of the Fabric of Santa Reparata and the Town Superintendent of the Works. Giotto also worked for Azzone Visconti in Milan and died 8th January 1337.

Virgin, Resurrection of the Virgin, and the *Assumption of the Virgin to Heaven on Christ's Throne*. Around the apse is a superb wooden carved inlay choir (1492-1501) with illustrious characters of the Order by Domenico da San Severino.

The central transept, also by Cimabue, shows the Evangelists writing their Gospels sat opposite the part of the World where according to tradition they wrote them. Matthew is with Judaea (lost in the earthquake of 1997), John with Asia, Mark with Italy, and Luke with Greece.

In the vault of the second bay from the transept are: *Jesus Christ*

Blessing, The Virgin Mary, St John the Baptist, and *St Francis.* In the crossing to the façade are the *Four Doctors of the Church*, the panel with St Jerome was also lost in the earthquake of 1997.

The fresco cycle continues in the nave with the scenes of the Old and of the New Testament. The episodes of the Old Testament are on the left of the altar, and on the right, as part of the history of humanity according to the old law a prefiguration of the new law, or rather the New Testament. Aloft, either side of the windows: the different days of *The Creation of the Universe*; *The Creation of Adam*; *The Creation of Eve from God's Rib*, to show that the Church will be born from the wound in the side of Jesus; *The Original Sin*, to symbolize the beginning of man's struggle against evil; *Expulsion from the Garden of Eden*, with the promise of redemption through the Son of God; *Tilling the Earth* (lost), atonement for sins; *The Sacrifice of Cain and Abel*, showing hate between human beings; *Murder of Abel* and *Cain Sent Away*, to show hate between men and their division into good and bad. Lower down is the painting of *The Construction of the Ark* to symbolise that the Church is the only means of salvation from evil; *The Flood*, a warning to those who think they can live without the Church; *Abraham and Isaac*, a prefiguration of the Sacrifice of Jesus, *The Angel Promises Adam the Lord's Blessing*; *Isaac Blesses Jacob*; *Isaac Prophesies to Esau his Atonement*; *Joseph is Sold by his Brothers*, a prefiguration of Jesus betrayed; *Joseph Forgives and Blesses his Brothers*, just as Jesus forgave his executioners.

In the nave over the entrance The *Pentecost* symbolizes the fulfilment of the divine plan in the foundation of the Church on earth. On the right wall, to the left of the viewer, are scenes of the New Testament. In the first bay, *The Annunciation, The Visitation, The Wedding at Cana* and *The Resurrection of Lazarus*; in the second bay *The Nativity, The Adoration of the Magi, The Capture of Jesus* and *The Scourging;* in the third bay *The Circumcision, The Flight into Egypt, Calvary, Crucifixion*; in the fourth bay *Jesus Disputing with the Doctors, Baptism of Jesus, Deposition, The Three Marys at the Sepulchre.*

This spectacular history of faith, seen through the comprehensive pictorial sequence of scenes from the Bible, is completed with the life of St Francis who, throughout his life reflected the life of the Saviour, from his birth in a stable to the stigmata on Mount Verna.

Scenes from the Life of St Francis

The lower part of the nave wall, the humblest but also the part nearest and most visible to the faithful, also recounts the existence of the Saint in honour of whom the basilica was built. Here is the masterpiece of 14th century Italian painting: 28 panels, three for every bay, except that next to the entrance, underneath the gallery showing the life of St Francis. Commissioned by the Minister General of the Order, Brother Giovanni di Muro, the frescoes were produced by Giotto di Bondone between 1297 and 1299. Facing the altar, on the right are: 1) *Homage of a Simple Man,* 2) *St Francis Gives his Cloak to a Poor Man,* 3) *Vision of the Palace,* 4) *Miracle of the Crucifix at San Damiano,* 5) *Renunciation of Worldly Goods,* 6) *Dream of Innocent III,* 7) *Honorius III Approves the Rule of St Francis,* 8) *Vision of the Flaming Chariot,* 9) *Vision of Thrones,* 10) *The Demons Cast Out of Arezzo,* 11) *St Francis before the Sultan (Trail by Fire),* 12) *Ecstasy of St Francis,* 13) *Institution of the Crib at Greccio,* 14) *The Miracle of the Spring,* 15) *Sermon to the Birds,* 16) *Death of the Knight of Celano,* 17) *St Francis Preaches before Pope Honorius III,* 18) *Apparition to the Chapter at Arles,* 19) *St Francis Receives the Stigmata,* 20) *Death and Ascension of St Francis,* 21) *Apparition to Brother Augustine and to Bishop Guido of Assisi,* 22) *The Noble Girolamo Verifies the Stigmata,* 23) *St Francis is Mourned by St Clare and the Poor Clares,* 24) *Canonisation of St Francis is,* 25) *Dream of St Gregory IX,* 26) *St Francis Heals a Nobleman,* 27) *St Francis Raises a Dead Woman,* 28) *The Liberation of the Heretic Pietro d'Alife.*

Worthy of note are the stained glass windows, considered among the most beautiful in Italy, by various 15th and 16th century artists. The windows illustrate various episodes of the life of the Saints. Leaving the Basilica the visitor will be able to enjoy the simplicity of the façade.

It is essential and stripped of all decoration and in the centre there is a single door with two openings to allow the flow of the faithful. Above is a rose window surrounded by the symbols of the four Evangelists: the Angel of St Matthew, the Ox of St Luca, the Lion of St Mark and the Eagle of St John to stress that the Franciscan Church only preaches the pure Gospel.

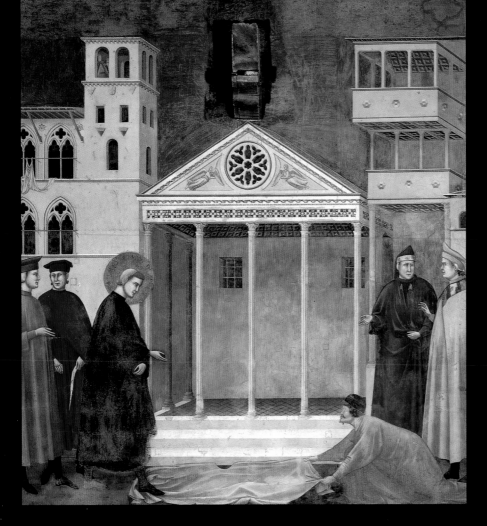

1) A man of Assisi he was… and whenever he met Francis…he would sweep the city streets before him and lay down his cloak, and place it under his feet…

From St Bonaventura's *Legenda Maior*.

2) He met a noble knight, but he was poor and badly dressed, Francis took pity on him, took off his cloak and, for the love of God, gave it to the poor knight.

3) He had a vision of a beautiful palace full of wonderful armour that God showed him for the compassion he had shown to the poor knight.

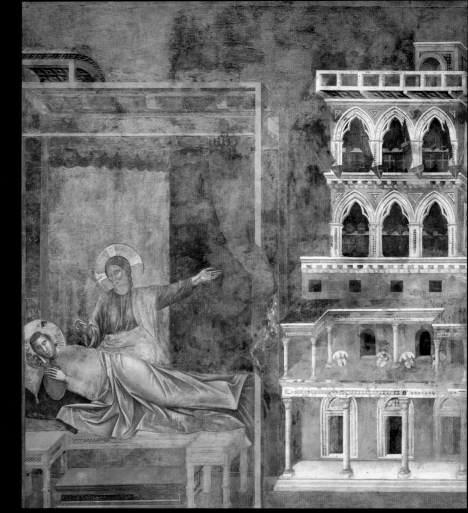

4) … having left the fields and gone out to the old dilapidated church of San Damiano,…he heard a divine voice which said, "Francis, go and repair my church you see all in ruins"

5) … so humble he stripped off his clothes and returned them to his father renouncing his inheritance… and said: "Up to now I have called you my father on earth, but from now on I will only say, "Pater noster qui es in coelis" (Our Father who art in Heaven)

6) … the Pope… had another dream in which he saw the church of St John Lateran about to fall, and a humble, scorned man who supported the church on his shoulders so that it wouldn't fall.

7) … and the Pope accepted the petition of the Blessed Francis and did everything he asked and loved him and promised to grant whatever he needed…

8) … they saw a flaming chariot, and went in the house, and three times went here and there, and above was a youth shining so brightly that it lit up the night sky like the day

9) This holy friar, Leo, who to be sleeping, saw a beautiful throne in heaven adorned with precious stones and all glory among other thrones but this one was empty… then he heard a voice which said, "This is Lucifer's chair, but he fell from Heaven to Hell because of his pride, and now this Throne is reserved for the humble Francis"

10) … the Blessed Francis was staying outside the city of Arezzo and over the walls of that city he saw a great horde of demons trying to create havoc… and so he sent his companion, Sylvester… to the city gates and said, "Tell those Demons that in obedience to God they are to leave"

11)… if you have doubts about leaving the faith of Mohammed for that of Christ, call for a great fire and let your holy men enter the fire with me, whoever is saved will believe in the other's faith…

12)… he was seen at night, praying, entranced with open arms, like a cross, surrounded by a shining cloud.

13)Giovanni da Greccio said and affirmed he had seen the little boy in the arms of the Blessed Francis, seeming to sleep and he was awoken by the Blessed Francis.

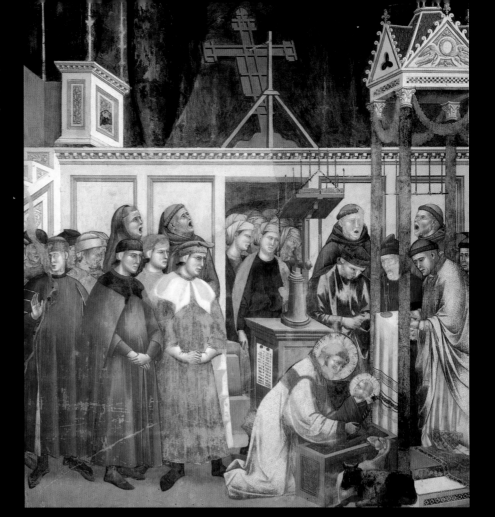

14)The Blessed Francis got down from the donkey and threw himself into prayer with his arms raised to the sky and said to the thirsty poor man, "Go to that stone and you will find running water that God in His mercy has given"

5) My brothers, praise God that He created you and dressed you in feathers to fly and conceded the purity of the air and given you reason to live.

6) They went into the refectory and began eating, the knight then passed out of this life at once, just as the Blessed Francis had envisaged.

7) … he raised his eyes to the sky and invoked the grace of the Holy Ghost, who gave him much understanding and such a voice that it moved the Pope and the Cardinals.

18) … the friars were at a Chapter at Arles and Brother Anthony from Padua, and the noble preaching friar Brother Monaldo saw through the Grace of God, the Blessed Father Francis raised in the air with his arms held open as if he were on a cross blessing the friars.

19) … a Seraphim came down from the sky… of such great splendour that it appeared to be burning… and within the wings of the Seraphim there seemed to be a crucified man… two wings were over the man's head, two spread out as if in flight and the other two were wrapped around his whole body.

20) and a friar… saw his soul as clear as a shining star, surrounded by a white cloud which took it straight to Heaven there to rest with Christ, its spouse…

21)… the night St Francis died, the Bishop of Assisi, who was on a pilgrimage to Monte Gargano had a vision of the Saint… while near Naples, the minister of the Friars, named Augustine, who had been dumb for years, was ill and close to death… cried out and said "Wait for me father, wait for me, I am coming to you…"

22) Jerome, the noble knight, doubted the miracle of the stigmata of the Blessed Francis… being more important than the others saw and touched and moved the nails with his hands, in the presence of many of clergymen and laymen who were there…

23) … solemnly going towards the city of Assisi, passing by the church of San Damiano, where the Noble virgin Clare lived… they rested a while. With her holy virgin sisters they were consoled to see and kiss the holy body of their father, the Blessed Francis…

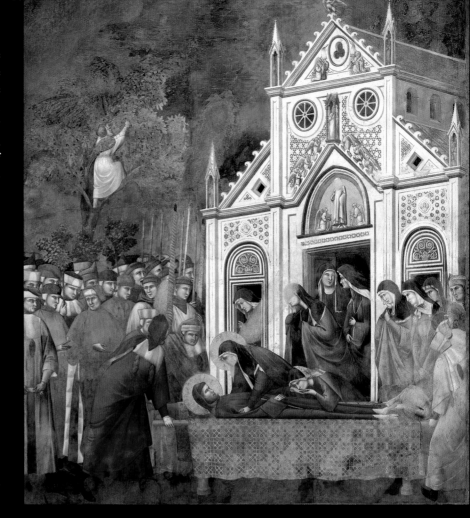

24) … and thus came the Pope with great solemnity and canonized him.

25) Pope Gregory was not without some doubt in his heart about the lance wound of Christ in his side. So, one night... the Blessed Francis appeared in dream, reproached him for his doubt, lifted his right arm and showed him the wound in his side.

26) ... a man called Giovanni... had a wound in his shoulder and another in the throat so great that the breath which came out was enough to put out six candles together... and then a man came through the window dressed as a Friar Minor... He dressed his wounds and... he was freed from illness and healthy.

27) The dead woman arose from her bed and calling one of the clergy hither …. said: Father, I want to confess, hear my sin.

28) … the Heretic Pietro d'Alife of Assisi was freed but was so amazed that he didn't know how to run away and stood at the doorway shouting, alarming his warders… his chains were taken before the Pope… who seeing what had happened, full of admiration blessed God.

Upper Church. Façade.

Museum-Treasure of the Basilica

The Museum has a collection of works of art of great historic and artistic value in rooms on the north side of the Great Cloister.

Refined goldsmith's work, tapestries, reliquaries and religious objects, such as chalices and crucifixes, can be admired.

The Museum also houses the precious Perkins collection, given to the Basilica in 1955 by the American art historian Frederik Perkins who, in his house in Assisi had put together a series of paintings of artistic value, including: *The Lady of the Milk* by Andrea di Bartolo, *St Francis of Assisi* by Fra Angelico, *The Lady of the Humility* by Lorenzo Monaco, a *Madonna with Child* attributed to Masolino da Panicale, and four pieces by Pietro Lorenzetti: *Madonna with Child, Madonna Enthroned with the Child, The Bishop's Funeral* and *Saint Cecilia*, all produced around 1340.

Masseo

Brother Masseo was the subject of a number of verses ("Fioretti") which had the theme of humility and obedience. He was an ambassador of St Francis to Sylvester and Clare whom he had asked to pray to discover the God's will. Masseo was with Francis in Rome when they prayed to the Apostles Peter and Paul for the gift of being able to live according to the Gospel in poverty. St Francis showed Brother Angelo and him the stigmata he had received on Mount Verna. Brother Masseo was with Francis when the saint asked for the Indulgence of Forgiveness for the Porziuncola. Masseo is also buried in the crypt in Basilica of St Francis.

Upper Church. Rose Window.

View of the Convent.

The Town

Leaving the Upper Church towards the Old Town go along Via San Francesco which offers varied architecture of medieval houses and elegant 16th century palazzi. At number 19, on the right, is the 15th century façade of **Palazzo Sperelli**, one of the noblest families of Assisi. On the left is the **Loggia by the Como Masters**, formerly the seat of the Corporation of Stone Masons from Como, built between the 13th and 15th centuries, embellished on the façade by ancient emblems.

Continuing along street is the **Pilgrims Oratory**, built in 1457 as a Hospice for travellers and run by the Confraternity of Saints James and Anthony the Abbot. On the façade is a fresco by Umbrian artist, Matteo da Gualdo. The inside of the Oratory is a veritable showcase of art entirely by artists of the calibre of Mezzastris, Pier Antonio da Foligno (1435-1506),

The Coat-of-Arms of Assisi.

Via San Francesco. Loggia of the Como Masters (detail).

and Matteo da Gualdo (1430-1530). The altarpiece is by Matteo da Gualdo with, in the centre the *Virgin Mary Enthroned with the Christ Child*, flanked by the titular Saints of the Oratory: *St Anthony* on the right, with his traditional piglet, and, on the left, by *St James*. On the right wall are two frescos by Mezzastris of the two miracles of St James: the hanged innocent youth saved by St James and the miracle of the roast cockerels who came alive on the platter of the judge who had unjustly condemned the youth.

The left wall has two episodes of the life of St Anthony: The *Sermon to the Camels* sent to the Saint bearing food and the *Distribution of Alms to the Poor*. In the vault

Via San Francesco. Pilgrims' Oratory. *The Miracle of St James* (Mezzatris).

panels are the Four Doctors of the Church.

Leaving the Oratory, on the left, at number 8 Via San Francesco, is the 16th century Palazzo Bartocci-Bindagoli. Further along, on the right, is the **Portico of Monte Frumentario**, built in 1267, with a loggia with seven reduced arches. Inside are interesting fragments of frescos from the grotesque period. Then there is the **Oliveira Fountain** commissioned by the Assisi nobleman Oliviero Ludovici in 1570.

Another palazzo of note in Via San Francesco is the sturdy **Palazzo Giacobetti Vallemani** with its "loud" 16th century lowered balcony, today home to the Civic Art Gallery (previously in the Town Hall).

The visit to the Gallery begins with the section from the Town

Via San Francesco. Portico of Monte Frumentario.

La famiglia Sperelli

The founder of the family was Massio, the father of Ranieri Sperella who was alive in 1149. In 1240 Nanni Sperelli liberated Assisi from the siege of Frederick II, Niccolò was Bishop of Assisi in 1377, Ascanio and Francesco were successively bishops of San Severino in the 17th century. Giacomo was Field Marshall to Guidobaldo, Duke of Urbino in 1484 and Emilio was a colonel in the service of the House of della Rovere.

Via San Francesco. Oliveira Fountain.

Via San Francesco. Palazzo Vallemani Giacobetti (detail of the façade).

Hall with works of art including the impressive *Maestà* by the workshop of Giotto. Then comes the section from the Palazzo dei Priori with work by Dono Doni (1500-1575); the third section has decorations of the ancient city aedicules on display and pieces from religious confraternities, including an interesting standard by Niccolò di Liberatore (1430-1502), known as "the Alunno" (ie, "the pupil").

The visit continues with the section devoted to the Hospitals with three great works by Ottaviano Nelli, then there is a section with work from the monasteries and convents of Assisi.

Beyond the Seminar arch, along Via dell'Arco del Seminario, is an imposing building with spacious loggias, the result of 17th century transformations and the 13th century **St Stephen's Church**, where according to legend, the bells "cried" the agony and death of St Francis.

From Piazzetta Verdi, down the steps opposite the Metastasio Theatre, is Piazzetta Garibaldi with Palazzo Fiumi Roncalli and the **Oratory of San Francescuccio**, built

Via del Seminario. Loggia of the Archiepiscopal Seminary

Via Portica. Archelogical Museum.

in the 14th century. In the façade, over the door, is a large fresco of the institution of Forgiveness. The inside is richly decorated with 14th century frescoes, including a Crucifixion with Saints Leonard and Francis.

After Via Verdi is Via Portico and the entrance of the Archaeological Museum in the crypt of San Niccolò, an ancient medieval church which was demolished in 1926 to make space for the construction of the post office. This religious building was also closely linked to Franciscan history as, according to tradition, it was here, in 1209, that St Francis, with his friend Bernard da Quintavalle, found his vocation in the Gospels.

Today the Crypt houses the rich archaeological museum with a number of finds from Assisi and the surrounding area. The collection is composed of sarcophagi, funerary urns, gravestones, and an interesting epigraphic collection. Through the museum it is possible to reach an area beneath today's square and observe the old Roman flooring with the original water ducts and the outer wall.

In the town square, the site of former Roman forum, rises the façade of the **Temple of Minerva**, built between the 1st and 2nd centuries BC. The Temple is one of the best surviving examples of a Roman temple, with its six Corinthian order grooved shaft columns sat upon strong solid plinths. During the early Middle Ages the Temple was a church but in the 13th century it was used as the Town Hall and once more became a church in 1456. In 1539 it was entitled Santa Maria Sopra Minerva.

The inside was restructured by Giacomo Giorgetti in 1634 and, in the 18th century, Francesco Appiano decorated the vault with an iconographic theme based on the glory of St Phillip and the Cardinal and Theological Virtues.

St Stephen's. The Bell Tower.

San Francescuccio.

Palazzo del Capitano del Popolo (Palace of the Captain of the People). Samples for bricks.

54

Piazza del Comune. Temple of Minerva and the Palazzo del Capitano del Popolo.

Piazza del Comune. Palazzo dei Priori (Priors' Palace).

MARCELLVS
TVTVS TV
CVS GVBER
NATOR

Palazzo dei Priori. The Painted Vault (detail).

To the left of the Temple is the **Palazzo del Capitano del Popolo** (Palace of the Captain of the People), built in the 13th century but much restored in a neo-Gothic style 1927 and the nearby Torre del Popolo built in 1305. On the other side of the square is the **Palazzo dei Priori**, the seat of the prior's magistracy, documented from 1330. The Palazzo del Priore was built in phases between 1275 and 1493. On the façade are the coats-of-arms of 16th century prelates and, on the right, is the so-called "Volta Pinta", that is a "painted vault" decorated with grotesques in 1556.

The other architectural feature of the square is a fountain, which existed in 1303. However, the fountain we see today was completely rebuilt in 1762.

Passing under the arch of Via del'Arco del Priore we then come to the **Chiesa Nuova**, built in 1615 in an elegant late Renaissance style at the expense of the King Phillip III of Spain over what is thought to have been the house of St Francis.

Inside, from the left, is the Chapel of the Crucifix with the *History of Saint Clare* by Caesar Sermei and then the Chapel of St Bernard with relative histories of

Piazza del Comune. The Fountain.

Palazzo dei Priori (detail). 16th century coats-of-arms (in the centre, that of Pope Paul III Farnese).

the Saint, also by Sermei. Around the central dome are episodes of the life of St Francis by Vincenzo Giorgetti, the second chapel on the left of the main altar is dedicated to the Virgin with the *Lady of the Cord* by Andrea Polinori from Todi. On the right of the main altar is the Chapel of St Anthony with an 18th century altarpiece with Franciscan saints by Tomaso d'Ascoli.

Sermei's altarpiece of the *Dream of St Francis* is in the presbytery. The church leads to the so-called

Chiesa Nuova. Façade.

Chiesa Nuova. Andrea Polinori's *Madonna of the Cord* (detail).

carcere (ie, jail) of St Francis, the small cell where Francis was locked-up by his father.

To left of the Chiesa Nuova is one of the most meaningful places for the history of St Francis: the **Oratory of San Francesco Piccolino**, where according to popular tradition, St Francis was born. A legend recounts how Lady Pica was having some difficulty in giving birth to Francis and a pilgrim suggested she go to a stable and there she would be able to give birth. This stable then became today's suggestive small church.

St Rufinus Cathedral

From the Piazza del Coumne, along the medieval Via San Ruffino one comes to the Cathedral, dedicated to St Rufinus, the first bishop of Assisi. The façade is a masterpiece of Romanesque art.

The body of the Saint, which until 412 had lain in some other small church in the area, was disputed by Bishop Hugo and the people of As-

The Tau

Tau is a Greek and Hebrew letter which corresponds to the Latin "T". From the earliest times of the Christian Church Tau was used as a particular sign of devotion later to become, with St Francis of Assisi, an important support to mystic theology.

Popular belief saw in this symbol a miraculous means of avoiding illness.

In the Middle Ages, the Tau was worn as either a ring or as an amulet.

sisi. According to an ancient tradition, the dispute was settled, in favour of the people by a sort of tug-of-war contest with the coffin.

From its foundation in the early Middle Ages the church grew further still from 1036, when Hugo, Bishop of Assisi, granted the church cathedral status and in 1253 Pope Innocent IV consecrated the building.

The Cathedral may be divided into three superimposed levels. The lower part dates back to the 12th century and has a series of panels in which are three doors, with, on either side, lions and griffons. In the lunette of the main door is a bas-relief with Christ enthroned and the Virgin nursing St Rufinus. The lunette over the door on left has two lions with a vase, in the right side lunette there are two birds drinking from a bowl.

The lower part is separated from the middle section by a gallery of arches richly embellished with zoological decorations full of medieval symbolism. There are also three elegant rose windows. The central rose window, the largest of the

San Francesco Piccolino.

It was painted on parchments and on door posts to ward off the plague.

Thus, Francis was particularly fond of the Tau as it reminded him of his love for the Cross and so he adopted it as a badge: no sign that recalled the Cross was of little importance.

The Tau is a the symbol of conversion and a renouncing of property. "Convert, be marked with the sign of the Tau, become poor", this is poem the friars dedicated to Lady Poverty.

Piazza della Chiesa Nuova. The Parents of St Francis.

three, is encircled by the symbols of the Evangelists and below with three telamons. The Romanesque bell tower completes the monumental structure.

The third, upper part is of a latter period and has a large pediment with a large Gothic arch in the tympanum. The inside of the Church, with a nave and two side aisles, was restored in 1571 by Perugian architect Galeazzo Alessi.

The baptismal font at the beginning of the right aisle recalls other episodes of the life of St Francis. It was here that both Francis, Clare and the Emperor Frederick II were baptised.

St Francis would often preach here after his conversion and it was in here that Clare heard for the first time the words spoken to the faithful by St Francis. On the right is the Chapel of the Blessed Sacrament by Giacomo Giorgetti (1663) with themes concerning the Eucharist and on the right wall, *Hagar in the Desert*, *David Praying* and *Elia and the Angel*, on the left, *Tobias and the Angel*, *David Receives the Bread*, the *Sacrifice of Isaac*, in the apse is the *Nativity*, the *Last Supper* and the *Resurrection*.

There are other frescos attributed to Giorgetti, Carlone and Giovanni Antonio Grecolini in the apse.

St Rufinus Cathedral. Façade.

There is a *Last Supper* by Brother Emanuele from Como over the entrance.

In the church, on the right, is the altar of the Our Lady of Sorrows and to then that of St Francis a stucco decoration by Agostino Silva showing the Cardinal Virtues with a painting by Dono Doni, dated 1550 with *Christ in Glory and the Saints*. In the right transept the altar dedicated to St Vitale has a *Deposition from the Cross* (1563) by Dono Doni.

The well-carved wooden Choir (1520) is by Piergiacomo da San Severino. The body of St Rufinus is under the main altar. In the left arm of the transept there is another Crucifix by Dono Doni. In the left aisle, from the lower part, are: the altar of St Gaetano of Thiene, the altar of the Crucifix, the altar of the Virgin and the altar of St Emidio with 18th century work by Francesco Appiani including the interesting canvas dated 1752 of the *Trinity, the Virgin and Saints* interceding for Assisi, and the altar of Santa Maria della Consolazione. In

St Rufinus Cathedral. Rose Window.

St Rufinus Cathedral. Lions.

the nave either side of the entrance stand the statues of St Francis and Saint Clare by Giovanni Duprè (dated 1882) and by Amalia Duprè (dated 1888) respectively. To the right of the façade of the church is the entry to the crypt with the remains of 11th century paintings, a bishop's throne and a Roman sarcophagus.

The Capitular Museum (enter via the right aisle) contains mid-14th century frescoes attributed to Puccio Capanna removed from the old medieval church of a *Flagellation*, a *Crucifixion* and a *Deposition*. There are also works by Niccolò Alunno: *Crucifixion*, *Deposition* and *Flagellation*, in addition to a *Madonna with Child*, *St Bernardino* and *St Sebastian* by Matteo da Gualdo and a series of 16th and 17th century paintings by Lorenzo Doni and Caesar Sermei.

Sylvester

Sylvester was an elderly secular priest of Assisi from whom Francis obtained the stones needed to repair a church. After having seen Bernard give away all his belongings to the poor and follow St Francis, Sylvester became greedy and complained to Francis that he had not been paid adequately. Francis, felt sorry for him, as he was "corroded by avarice" and then filled his hand with money. Sylvester was impressed by such generosity and had a vision of seeing a gold cross coming from the saint's mouth. He then repented and left all his property to the Franciscan Order of which he was the first priest and in which he was to live a holy life for the rest of his days.

The Rocca Maggiore (Great Fortress).

The Rocca Minore (Fortress) and the Bell Tower of St James's.

Bernard da Quintavalle

Bernard, from a wealthy noble family, was the first of St Francis' followers. St Francis had often been a guest in Bernard's house and so had learned of the Saint's life and holiness. Two years after St Francis' conversion and much stimulated by the Saint's penitent life and deep prayer, Bernard told Francis of his intention to give away his possessions. The next morning, along with Pietro Cattani who had similar intentions, they went to the St Nicolò's Church. During a journey to the Pope in Rome (in 1209 or 1210), Bernard was elected as head of the group of twelve as "the vicar of Jesus Christ". In 1211 he was sent to preach at Bologna, Florence and Santiago de Compostela. Francis had predicted that Bernard would have been challenged by a series of temptations and tribulations, but that he would have weathered every storm and he would have overcome any hardship.

The Rocca Maggiore and the Rocca Minore

From Piazza San Ruffino the street on the right Via di Porta Perlici leads to the characteristic medieval quarter called Porta Perlici from which it is easy to reach the **Rocca Maggiore** (or Great Fortress) with its magnificent views over the city and the surrounding area.

The history of the Fortress dates back to 1173, when the city fell to Cristiano di Magonza, a *condottiere* in the army of Federico Barbarossa. The Rocca was destroyed during the turmoils of 1198 and rebuilt by Cardinal Albornoz in 1356. The Fortress is connected via the medieval walls to the other fortress, the **Rocca Minore** also built in the 14th century by Albornoz. Back in the Piazza del Comune, after having gone down Corso Mazzini with its elegant historical *palazzi* we come to Piazza **Santa Chiara**.

The Rocca Minore.

St Clare's

The façade of the Church dedicated to St Clare rises in its elegant simplicity in the 19th century square, later adorned by a fountain in 1872, from which a singular view of the Umbrian Valley may be enjoyed.

When St Francis died at the Porziuncola, the inhabitants of Assisi, while the new church dedicated to him was being built, brought his body back to the city to the church of St George where the body of Saint Clare was put after her death at San Damiano in 1253.

The church of St George, begun by Filippo di Campello (1257-1260), is on the site where Saint

St Clare's.

St Clare's. Master of St Clare, *St Clare*.

the Master of St Clare of the *Manger and the Madonna with Child*, higher up on the walls are scenes from the Book of Genesis. The noteworthy 13th century main altar is by a unknown local artist. In the apse is a marvellous *Crucifix* attributed to Giunta Pisano commissioned by Sister Benedetta, the first abbess of the convent after the death of Saint Clare in 1260. The frescos over the altar, by the School of Giotto, show, the *Virgin and Saint Clare*, *St Agnes Virgin and Martyr*, *Saint Catherine*, and *Saint Lucia*. In the right transept is another painting attributed to the Master of St Clare of *St Clare and the Stories of her Life*. In the right part of the crossing are scenes from the life of St Clare and from the New Testament, attributed to the Master of St Clare, namely: the *Annunciation to Joachim*, *The Marriage of the Vir-*

Clare was consecrated in 1265 by Pope Clement IV.

The light extremely linear façade is crossed by strips of white and pink stones and may be divided into three parts. The lunette, over the entrance with its round arch, has a ruined fresco by Giacomo Giorgetti. Lower down are two lions supporting the arch. Over the entrance is a sumptuous rose window.

On the left are three 14th century buttresses. With its cruciform plan and large vaulted nave, inside of the church is not unlike that of the Upper Church of the Basilica of St Francis. The first chapel on the left, with 20th century frescoes, is dedicated to Saint Agnes and contains the remains of the Blessed Amalia and the Blessed Benedetta.

In the left arm of the transept there is a 13th century painting by

St Clare's. *Crucifix of San Damiano*.

Santa Maria Maggiore. Façade.

Santa Maria Maggiore. *Our Lady of Mercy.*

gin, *The Slaughter of the Innocent,* *Flight into Egypt, Jesus Disputing with the Doctors,* and a *Last Judgment.*

On the right side of the aisle is the chapel of the Holy Sacrament, which backs onto the ancient church of St George, with a wealth of frescos attributed to Pace di Bartolo; on the side a *Madonna with Child* and *Saints* by Puccio Capanna and other frescos by the School of Giotto: a *Resurrection,* a *Deposition* and the *Entombing of Jesus in the Sepulchre.* From the chapel we now pass into the Oratory of the Crucifix. Over the altar is another 12th century *Crucifix* of rare beauty with extremely simple forms which, according to tradition, was that in the church of St Damiano which spoke to St Francis.

There are other frescos: *Saint Clare,* the *Madonna Enthroned, St Anne, St Jerome, St Rocco* and *St Francis* and a portrait of *Pope Urban V* by Pace di Bartolo.

The neo-Gothic crypt with the body of St Clare can be reached via the nave. The body was found in 1850 after eight nights continuous, untiring work and then placed in a crystal urn.

Santa Maria Maggiore

From St Clare's the church of **Santa Maria Maggiore** may be reached after a walk along Via Santa Agnese. Santa Maria Maggiore, (before St Rufinus, the first cathedral in Assisi) is in the Romanesque style with an extremely sober façade with just two pilasters to break its monotony.

The inside, with three aisles, has 14th century by Pace di Bartolo including an *Annunciation,* a *Madon-*

St Peter's. Façade.

Along Via Giovanni di Bonino is the monastery of the closed order of St Quiricus. Then, along Via di Sant'Appollinare is the other monastery of St Joseph.

St Peter's

The church of **St Peter** is in Viale di Borgo San Pietro. The church is a further example of an elegant Romanesque construction and consecrated by Innocent IV in 1253.

On the rectangular façade, divided into a lower and upper part by two lines of projecting arches, are three very beautiful rose windows and on either side of the entrance two lions stand guard. The inside, on three aisles has maintained the austere essentiality of the Romanesque structure as may been seen in the raised presbytery.

In the chapel to left of the apse are some traces of 13th century frescos. In the chapel of the Holy Sacrament, to the left of the presbytery are traces other 13th century frescos with an *Annunciation*, a *Christ in Majesty* and *St Vittorino*.

na with Child, a *Crowning of the Virgin* and a *Visitation*, and a *Pietà* attributed to Tiberio of Assisi. At the start of the nave there is an interesting 9th century sarcophagus.

Close to the church is the Bishop's Palace where, according to tradition, St Francis gave up his worldly goods and lived before his death before being taken to the Porziuncola.

Inside of Peter's (detail).

St Peter's. Apse wall.

San Damiano.

San Damiano. *Madonna with Child between St Clare and St Francis.*

In the chapel to left of the entrance is 17th century painting of *Our Lady of the Rosary*, and either side of the door are two *trecento* tombs. Along the walls of the are elegant medieval tombs, some of which are of the Sperelli family, and, on the right side, the sepulchre of the Blessed Antonio Pennacchi, a nobleman from Bettona.

San Damiano

Leaving through the Porta Nuova city gate along Corso Vittorio Emanuele, we come to one of the most important places, full of historical and religious meaning relative to the life of Saint Francis: the **Church and Convent of San Damiano**.

Originally, San Damiano was

San Damiano. St Jerome's Chapel. *The Virgin Enthroned and Saints* by Tiberio of Assisi.

just one of the many half abandoned chapels in the outskirts of Assisi, but it was here that in the summer of 1205, St Francis found shelter to pray in isolation and meditate before a Crucifix by one of Cimabue's forerunners.

It was this Crucifix that spoke to St Francis with the words: "Go Francis and repair my Church!". The Saint of Assisi interpreted literally the universal character of the message and, after having sold some personal belongings, repaired the small building.

In 1212 St Clare and her companions stayed here and so the first convent of the Poor Clares was founded next to the modest church of San Damiano. In 1224 St Francis, in deep pain and suffering from the wounds of the Stigmata, went to find shelter in San Damiano and the small reed hut the nuns had erected for him and it was then that he wrote his famous "Canticle of the Creatures" (or "Brother Sun").

St Clare's mother, Ortolana and her younger sisters, Agnes and Beatrice, joined Clare at San Dami-

San Damiano. Nave.

San Damiano. The Choir.

ano, which the Saint called the Porziuncola. Clare and her companions lived and strictly applied the rule of St Francis with an indissoluble love for Christ.

The church overlooks an attractive square with, to the right, an aedicule with a 15th century fresco of the *Virgin and Saints Francis and Clare.*

The façade is further embellished by a portico, to the right of which is the entrance to Chapel of St Jerome decorated by Tiberio of Assisi with frescos of the *Virgin Mary, Saints Clare and* **Francis Bernardino** *and Jerom*e. The single nave church has maintained its original state of poverty and simplicity. On the immediate right hand side of the entrance is the window from which, according to popular tradition, the young Francis threw the money refused by the priest of San Damiano for the repair of the Church.

The episode is recalled by the relative 14th century fresco of the XIV with the Saint praying, offering money and being chased by his father. The painting of St Agnes, to

the right the chapel of the Crucifix, a pleasant 17th century work by Brother Innocent from Palermo with a particularity: Christ's expression changes with the position of the viewer.

Above the altar is a copy of the crucifix that spoke to St Francis, the original of which is in St Clare's Church. In the centre of the 16th

century choir is a grille through which Clare and his sisters received Holy Communion. In the apse is *Madonna with Child, St Damian* and *St Rufinus*. On the left wall of the nave are some 16th century paintings in a poor state of repair showing the *Funeral of Saint Clare.*

To the right of the altar is the vestibule under which are entombed all the Poor Clares who died before Clare; to left is the choir with the relative 13th century wooden stalls and a *Crucifixion* by Pier Antonio Mezzastris dated 1482.

Through the vestibule up some small steps is the garden of Saint Clare from which there is wide panorama of the plain below. Further up is the Saint's Oratory with 14th century frescoes and, further still, are the nuns' dormitories. There is a cross on the wall which marks the place where on 11 August 1253 St Clare ended her holy existence.

The steps lead back down to one of the most beautiful Franciscan cloisters with some frescos by Eusebio da San Giorgio dating back to 1507: *St Francis Receives the Stig-*

San Damiano. The Refectory.

View of Santa Maria degli Angeli from San Damiano.

San Damiano. The Cloister.

mata and an *Annunciation*. Access to the Refectory is through the cloister. The Refectory has also remained unchanged in its primitive simplicity, with some original tables from the time of Saint Clare, whose seat is marked by a white cross.

Saint Clare and the Poor Clares

Clare was born in Assisi in 1194, the daughter of the noble Favarone di Offreduccio and Ortolana Fiumi. Shortly before Clare was born, her mother had gone to pray in Cathedral where she heard a mysterious voice say, "Oh woman fear not because you will happily give birth to a bright light that will illuminate the world".

Clare was born and then baptised in the Cathedral of St Rufinus. The deeply religious upbringing and soul open to God soon led to Clare being attracted to the message of poverty preached by Francis. The 18th March 1212 Clare secretly went to the Porziuncola where Francis invested her in the Franciscan habit and, after having cut her hair, consecrated her to the Lord.

Francis later took her to the Benedictine nuns at Bastia and from there she was temporarily moved to St Angelo di Panzo on the eastern slopes of Mount Subasio. Clare was joined in this latter convent by her sister Agnes thus further exasperating the family of the two sisters.

But Clare's vocation did not lie in the Benedictine Order and so she went to the small convent next to the small church of San Damiano that St Francis had repaired. She lived there for 42 years up to her

San Damiano. Fresco in the Oratory of St Clare (detail).

JACOPA

Jacopa (or Giacoma or Giacomina [ie, Jacqueline]) de Settesoldi, no longer a young woman, was the widow of Graziano Frangipani a nobleman from Rome. Francis met Jacopa in Rome in 1219 during one of his sermons. Lady Jacopa would take Francis around Rome much as she would have done with her own children.

From then on she became one of the most generous benefactors of the Franciscan Order in Rome. It was through Jacopa that the Order obtained the Hospital of St Biagio from the Benedictines. St Biagio then became the first Roman site of the Franciscans with the name of San Francesco a Ripa.

Despite being active and resolute, devout and affectionate, Jacopa could almost be described as a man. Indeed, while Francis would call Clare his sister, he would call Jacopa brother.

Before dying Francis wanted Jacopa at his bedside and had her come from Rome. When in Rome Jacopa would bring Francis cloth, wax and food and biscuits made from flour and honey called "mostaccioli". That last time Francis also asked her to bring a sheet, wax for the funeral and those "things to eat" that she had prepared for Francis when he was ill in Rome.

After the death of St Francis, Jacopa never left Assisi. She stayed near his tomb and dedicated herself to charitable and pious works. She followed Francis to the grave 13 years later and was first entombed in the Church of San Giorgio and later in a new tomb in the Basilica of St Francis.

death having founded the second Franciscan Order which initially took the name of the Order of the Poor secluded Ladies of St Damian, or of the Poor Sisters, called the Poor Clares only after the death of their founder.

Clare was confined to bed for most of the last years of her life for an illness she had contracted in 1224. The night of Christmas 1252 Clare was lying down in her dormitory while her sisters had gone down to the chapel to pray, when she suddenly heard singing in the far off church of St Francis and saw the Christ Child in the manger swaddled in light.

In 1958, in memory of that prodigious vision Pope Pius XII, proclaimed St Clare the patron saint of television. She died the evening of 11th August 1253 and was canonized in 1255.

The life style of the first nuns followed that of the Friars Minor keeping to a strict principle of poverty which forbade accepting money and goods under any form whatsoever.

The Poor Clares vowed complete obedience to the Church and a life of total seclusion and isolation.

Convents of Poor Clares quickly spread throughout Italy with increasing numbers of women who abandoned a secular life for a religious monastic one.

The initial rigours of the rule had, in the meantime, been somewhat more relaxed and the Order of the Poor Clares, the Second Order, also had to follow the Observance.

The convents which adhered still refused to possess property but most followed the custom of accepting a dowry from postulants.

Santa Maria di Rivotorto

Further down from San Damiano is the neo-Gothic church of Santa Maria di Rivotorto, built in 1854 over the site were St Francis drew up the First Rule. The façade bears the wording "Qui ebbe inizio l'Ordine dei Minori" ("The Order of Friars Minor started here"). Francis came to this church in 1209 with his two disciples, Bernard da Quintavalle and Pietro Cattani, living in absolute poverty and begging for alms.

Inside the church, the ancient hovel with the bed of the "Poverello", the chapel and the kitchen were reconstructed in 1926.

San Damiano. *St Clare*.

Santa Maria di Rivotorto.

The Hermitage of the Carcere.

Leo

Brother Leo witnessed the Saint's prayer and his ecstasies. He was at Fonte Colombo when Francis rewrote the Rule and received Elia and other ministers. He was also at La Verna when Francis received the stigmata. Francis wrote to Leo and received a written blessing from the Saint. Brother Leo was present at the death of both St Francis and Saint Clare. He also had visions of many Franciscan friars not keeping to the rule of poverty. He died in 1271 and is buried near the tomb of St Francis in the crypt of the Basilica of St Francis.

Pietro Cattani

He chose the habit of the penitents with Bernard, the jurist and canon of San Rufino, and was a companion of St Francis on his voyage to the East. In 1220 at the Chapter-General held in the Porziuncola, St Francis, in front of all friars gathered there resigned all his official positions in the Order saying, "From this day hence I am dead for you. But here is Brother Pietro di Cattani whom you and I must obey". Pietro died in 1221 at the Porziuncola.

The Hermitage of the Carcere

The Hermitage of the Carcere (or Cells) is just 4 kilometres from the Capuchins. Another historic place closely tied to Franciscan spirituality. Here, Francis and his followers retreated for long periods in prayer and in isolation in order to fortify the spirit.

At the *carcere* (cell or prison), the Saint, who was by now blind, went out to search for Brother Bernard who was in prayer in the woods, but the friar did not answer, then, Francis heard the voice of God who said, "Oh, poor little man, what torments you so? When you called, Brother Bernard was with me and could not come to answer you". The building is extremely simple but at the time of St Francis everything was probably humbler still, as both the cloister and the convent had been built in the 15th century by St Bernardino of Siena. The area is completely surround by woods, immersed in uncontaminated nature of rare beauty.

The altarpiece is a 15th century fresco of the *Crucifixion*.

The entrance to the tiny oratory, almost certainly the remains of the first church dedicated to St Mary of the Cells, is in the right wall.

The Grotto of St Francis, where the saint would pray is under the sacristy. The Grotto still has the saint's bed of stone and on the wall there is a 13th century fresco of the Sermon to the Birds. This is possibly where the birds would come to perch on the tree to listen to St Francis.

Another event of the saint's life in this building concerns the so-called "Devil's Hole" where the demon fell because of the power of St Francis' prayers. The crevice, or hole, is still clearly visible today.

Further along Viale di San Francesco, there are other caves were the saint's companions would isolate themselves in prayer, the grottoes of the Blessed Sylvester, the Blessed Bernard, the Blessed Leo, and the Blessed Giles (Egidio).

The Hermitage of the Carcere. Detail.

Santa Maria degli Angeli and the Porziuncola

The Basilica of Santa Maria degli Angels was built between 1569 and 1684, by Pope St Pius V to protect the Porziuncola and to accommodate the numerous pilgrims who flocked to these holy places. It was originally a small chapel where it was said angels could be heard singing.

The greatest architects of the age competed to design the Church including Galeazzo Alessi, Girolamo Martelli and the Vignola (Jacopo Barozzi).

Earthquakes and collapses meant there had to be many repairs and restorations of the original structure and it was not until 1928 that the façade was produced by architect Caesar Bazzani. At the top of the façade is the majestic statue of the Virgin, the caused of fervent devotion for its miraculous movements in 1948.

The church has a nave and two side aisles. In the first chapel of the right aisle, dedicated to St Anthony the Abbot, there is a picture of the Saint by Giacomo Giorgetti dated 1670 and there are some frescoes by Francesco Appiani. The second chapel, dedicated to St John the Baptist is decorated by frescos by Caesar Sermei with scenes of the life of the Baptist. The third chapel, dedicated to St Anne, has frescoes (dated 1602) by Antonio Circignani (known as the Pomarancio) with the stories of Virgin. The fourth chapel, dedicated to St Pius V Ghislieri, has an altarpiece by Baldassarre Croce, author of the fresco of the *Ecstasy of Pope Pius V*. The fifth chapel, of the Annunciation, shows the *Procession of the Veil of the Virgin,* the original façade of the Basilica can be seen in this work.

In the right arm of the transept is the altar of St Peter in Chains by Jean Reinhold in 1675 with, on either side, the altar of St Peter of Alcantara, with a picture of *Christ with St Peter of Alcantara and St Margherita from Cortona* by Francis Appiani (1757), and of the Reli-

Santa Maria degli Angeli. Façade.

Angelo

Brother Angelo was one of the three authors (with Leo and Rufinus) of the letter of Greccio. Angelo is buried in the crypt in Basilica of St Francis.

Leo is mentioned in the list of virtues of the perfect friar for his courtesy.

He was the first knight to enter the Order and was full of kindness. Angelo was Francis' guard at Montecasale and on many other occasions in the life of the Saint. Angelo was also present when Francis received the stigmata during Lent in 1224 on Mount Verna.

Brother Angelo was one of the four companions (with Bernard, Leo and Rufinus) who assisted Francis during his last illness.

Giles (Egidio)

Giles comes after Bernard and Pietro in the list of the first followers of St Francis in a life of penitence. Born in Assisi, in 1208, Giles was "gladly" welcomed at the Porziuncola by Francis who saw in him faith and kindness. Giles preached with Francis in the Ancona Marches and went to Santiago de Compostela with Bernard. Brother Giles was also with the dying St Francis. "A simple man, upright and God-fearing, throughout his life he practised saintliness, justice and piety leaving examples of perfect obedience, manual labour, and a love for religious meditation and contemplation". Despite being illiterate and simple, Giles reached the highest levels of contemplation. In the list of virtues of the perfect friar, Giles is remembered for his "high thoughts of contemplation ... reaching the highest perfection".

The Porziuncola.

quary respectively. In the pendentives of the dome there is a series of frescoes by Francesco Appiani: *St Francis founds the Order Friars Minor*, the *Benedictines Cede the Porziuncola to St Francis*, the *Investiture of St Clare* and *St Bonaventure writing the Life of the Saint*. Standing out under the centre of the transept, protected by the large dome is the small poor oratory of the Porziuncola (which means "small portion of ground"). The humble building within the sumptuous church towering above provokes, in the careful eye of the faithful, an evident sense of contrast.

The Porziuncola was originally a modest Benedictine chapel called the Blessed Mary of Jehoshaphat which, according to an ancient tradition, was erected by pilgrims returning from the Holy Land.

On his return from Rome, after the Pope had approved the Order, Francis stayed in this dilapidated building where, since 1208, he had begun to gather with his companions. Francis asked the Benedictine monks for permission to settle in

Chapel of the Roses. *Life of St Francis* (detail).

this cramped ruined dwelling without however, buying it or having it given to him, but he would have paid a crate of dace caught in the Teschio River.

The Porziuncola became the permanent abode of the new Franciscan Order, the place where meetings were held, missions were organised and the friars would pray in seraphic joy. From Pentecost of 1215 all the Chapters-General of the Order were held here, up to the most famous one in 1221 when 5,000 Franciscans participated. The large numbers called for additional matting (*stuoie*) to be made to accommodate the all the friars and so the Chapter-General became known as the "Chapter of the Mats".

St Francis, who was by then very ill, passed away on the 3rd October 1226 surrounded by a flock of warbling swallows. And in the Porziuncola, on the night of 18th March 1212, Francis consecrated the eighteen year-old Clare to the service of God. She then founded the Second Franciscan Order called the Poor Secluded Ladies of St Damian, subsequently known as the Poor Clares. In July 1216 obtained God's intercession The Saint in July 1216, through the intercession of the Virgin Mary, obtained the God's indulgence of Forgiveness for all those who had visited the Church with contrite hearts.

The present building has partly been modified and has lost its original form of a poor rural church.

A fresco dated 1830 covers the façade and has *St Francis Asking for the Indulgence of Foregiveness*, by Friedrich Overbeck of Lubeck, while on the outside rear wall there is a *Crucifixion* by Perugino (Pietro Vannucci). The inside with its ogive vault has maintained its austere but serene character and it is still possible to pray in front of the large painting by Ilario da Viterbo of the *Annunciation* (1393) with scenes concerning Forgiveness. The paintings on the vault of the *Evangelists* and the *Immago Pietatis* on the left wall have both been attributed to Ilario da Viterbo.

On the right, of the beginning of the presbytery, is the Chapel of the Transitus, this was the infirmary where St Francis died on the bare earth. After his beatification it was transformed into a chapel.

On the outside wall there is a fresco by Domenico Bruschi of 1886 showing the death and funeral of the Saint. On the inside are some frescoes by Giovanni di Pietro, known as "Spagna", dated 1516, with saints and blessed Franciscans. The beautiful enamelled terracotta statue of St Francis over the altar is by Andrea della Robbia. In the lower part of the apse is an imposing 17th century wooden choir. Under the main altar is the crypt and a terracotta reredos by Andrea della Robbia with six scenes of the Saint's life.

In the left arm of the transept is the altar of St Anthony of Padua with a wooden 17th century crucifix. On the left is the altar of the Virgin and the Graces with the icon of Our Lady of Philermos, protectress of the ancient Order of the Knights of Malta. The Oratory of the Sacrament is reached via the transept on the right. Here there are frescoes from the Porziouncola by the Perugino, the *Annunciation* and the *Virgin*. On the altar is the Ciborium from Santa Chiara.

Returning to the chapels, in the left aisle is the Chapel of the Rosary with paintings by Domenico Muratori and Baldassarre Orsini and frescoes by Carlo Ventura Morelli. The fourth chapel, dedicated to the Coronation of the Virgin, was decorated by Simeone Cimurri in 1603 with

Chapel of the Transitus. *Death of St Francis* (Domenico Bruschi).

Santa Maria degli Angeli. Gilded bronze statue of the Virgin Mary.

The Rose Garden. St Francis and the Wolf of Gubbio.

Giacomo Giorgetti
(1603-1679)

Giorgetti was the pupil of Sermei and Lanfranco. He worked at Assisi, at Perugia, in the Cloister of San Francesco al Prato, and at Foligno, where nothing remains of his activity. Among his last work, at Assisi, is St Anthony the Abbot in Santa Maria degli Angeli, very much in the style of Lanfranco.

Cesare Sermei
(1581-1668)

The son of artist Ferdinando Sermei from Orvieto, Cesare Sermei is remembered for his work at Assisi, and from the mid 17th century onwards he worked in other Umbrian centres. Sermei was strictly tied to a rigid pictorial mould, even ancient ones, such as those of Giotto, Alunno, Signorelli and Spagna. Although most of his work was in Assisi, his work elsewhere is also worthy of mention, such as the paintings in vault of the Maddalena Church and in the Oratory of Nobles in Perugia, and in the Vici Chapel in the Montesanto Monastery at Todi.

Santa Maria degli Angeli. The Cloister (detail).

the *Assumption of the Virgin*, *St Diego Heals the Son of the King of Spain*, *Apparition of Saints Francis and Clare*. Next is the Chapel of the Deposition with work by Baldassarre Croce and Piergirolamo Crispolti depicting the *Christ's Farewell* and the *Risen Christ*, the vault has frescoes by the Sienese Ventura Salimbene of *Saint Clare Dying* and the *Risen Christ*.

The second to last chapel, the so-called Stigmata Chapel, has work relative to the Stigmata by Giacomo Giorgetti, *St Francis Receives the Stigmata*, *Verification of the Stigmata,* and by Caesar Sermei with *Saint Clare Greeting St Francis* and, in the vault, *Approval of the Rule*. The last chapel is dedicated to St Diego of Alcalà with paintings by Ippolito da Coceto, Baldassarre Orsini and Giovanni Cavallucci.

The Sacristy is reached through the Chapel of the Transitus. The Sacristy is furnished with 17th century cupboards with lunettes painted with saints and Franciscan histories by Girolamo Martelli. From here the visitor can enter the Rose Garden. It was here that St Francis was tempted one night by the Devil, and trying to ward off instincts of his body, went out from his cell and, totally naked, threw himself into a rose bush which miraculously lost its prickly thorns. Nearby is the **Chapel of the Roses**, divided into three rooms on the walls of which are scenes of the life of St Francis by Tiberio of Assisi in 1518, the *Saint Throws Himself into the Rose Bush*, the *Saint is Led to the Porziuncola by Two Angels*, *Asking God for the Indulgence of Forgiveness*, the *Pope Confirms the Rule*, *Publication of Indulgence*.

In a following room there are other frescoes by Tiberi: *St Francis and his First Companions*, *Saint Clare and Saint Elisabeth*, *St Bonaventure, Bernardino from Siena, Louis from Toulouse* and *Anthony from Padua*. Beneath the chapel is the cell where the Saint recited his prayer when he was tempted by the Devil. The two beams supporting the ceiling are the only remains of the pulpit from which the Indulgence of Forgiveness was promulgated.

Outside, in a small garden, the fig tree recalls the episode of when St Francis asked the cricket to sing for eight days. Next, through a cloister, is a small 15th century convent. The convent is now a five-room museum with a collection of various artefacts of sacred art.

In the second room there is a *Crucifix* (1236) by Giunta Pisano and another painting of St Francis (1250) by the Master of St Francis. The third room leads to the staircase, which in turn leads to the upper floor where it is possible to visit the rooms of the old convent and to admire a *Pietà* (1508) on the wall at the end of the corridor.

The Feast Days of Assisi

The *Calendimaggio*

This is when the whole city takes a step back in time and the population dresses in medieval and renaissance costume. The *Calendimaggio* takes place the first Thursday, Friday and Saturday in May. The celebration begins with the blessing of the flags in the Basilica of St Francis and the Cathedral of St Rufinus. In Piazza del Comune the Master of the Field assumes the sovereign powers he holds throughout the celebrations. There is a competition between the two halves of the city: the "Parte de Sotto" and the "Parte de Sopra". A jury then decides which side was best able to recreate the historical settings with costumes, songs, games and displays of skill. The winner then receives the Pallium: the "Palio".

Feast of Forgiveness

This important religious feast is celebrated in August at Santa Maria degli Angeli at Porziuncola to recall the time when, in July 1216, St Francis obtained, through the intercession of the Virgin, God's the great *Perdono d'Assisi*, more commonly known as the "Portiuncula Indulgence" for the remission of sins for all those who had visited, confessed and received Holy Communion in the Franciscan church. This high privilege was confirmed by Pope Honorius III.

Feast of the Vow

Solemn celebrations are held in June to remember the liberation from the Saracens thanks to the intercession of St Clare. Frederick II had positioned a number of Saracen archers near the city and one day ferocious troops broke into the city near the church of San Damiano but St Clare who was then sick on her deathbed ordered her sisters to place her in front of the door of the convent. She then invoked Divine Protection and the Saracen Army fled.

The *Calendimaggio*.

The *Calendimaggio*.

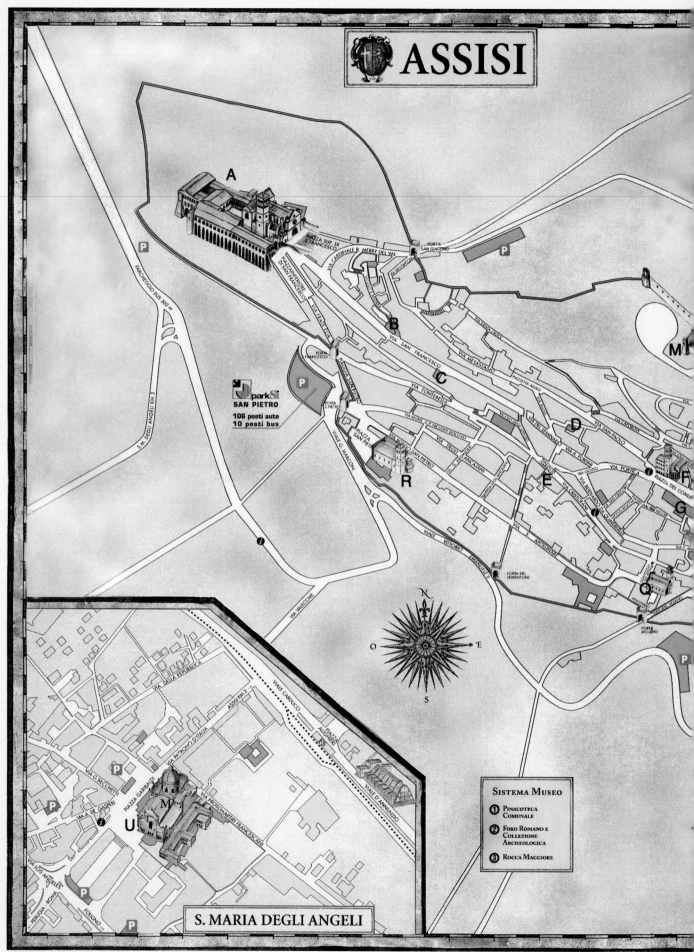

ASSISI

SISTEMA MUSEO

1 PINACOTECA COMUNALE

2 FORO ROMANO E COLLEZIONE ARCHEOLOGICA

3 ROCCA MAGGIORE

S. MARIA DEGLI ANGELI

Many thanks to Consorzio Albergatori ed Operatori Turistici di Assisi

Legend

A - The Basilica of St Francis
B - Loggia of the Como Masters
C - Pilgrims' Oratory
D - St Stephen's Church
E - Oratory of San Francescuccio
F - Palazzo del Capitano del Popolo and the Temple of Minerva
G - Palazzo dei Priori
H - Chiesa Nuova
I - Oratory of San Francesco Piccolino
L - St Rufinus Cathedral
M - Rocca Maggiore (Great Fortress)
N - Rocca Minore
O - The Hermitage of the Carcere
P - St Clare's Church
Q - Santa Maria Maggiore
R - St Peter's Church
S - San Damiano
T - Santa Maria di Rivotorto
U - Santa Maria degli Angeli and the Porziuncola

Information

Assisi Tourist Information
(Comuni di Assisi, Bastia Umbra, Bettona, Cannara)
P.zza del Comune - 06081 Assisi
Tel. 075812534 - Fax 075813727
E-mail: info@iat.assisi.pg.it

Useful Numbers

Town Hall	07581381
Carabinieri (Police)	075812376
Red Cross	0758043059
Hospital	075816342
Taxi	075813193

Museums

Roman Forum and Archaeological Collection
Via Portica - tel. 075813053
16 ottobre – 15 marzo 10/13 14/17
16 marzo – 15 ottobre 10/13 15/19

Art Gallery
Via San Francesco, Palazzo Vallemani
tel. 075812033
16 ottobre – 15 marzo 10/13 14/17
16 marzo – 15 ottobre 10/13 14/18

Rocca Maggiore
tel. 075813053
10/18.

Hotels

★★★★ GRAND HOTEL ASSISI
Via F.lli Canonichetti
Tel. 07581501 - Fax 0758150777

★★★★ LE SILVE
Loc. Caparrocchie - Fraz. Armenzano
Tel. 0758019000 - Fax 0758019005

★★★★ SUBASIO
Tel. 075812206 - Fax 075816691

★★★ ABACUS
Via E. Berlinguer - Fraz. S. Maria Angeli
Tel. 0758043940 - Fax 0758043948

★★★ ANTONELLI FRANCO
Via Los Angeles, 25 - Fraz. S. Maria Angeli
Tel. 0758043690 - Fax 0758048028

★★★ CASTEL S. GREGORIO
Via S. Gregorio, 16 - Fraz. S. Gregorio
Tel. 0758038009 - Fax 0758038904

★★★ CRISTALLO
Via Los Angeles, 195
Fraz. S. Maria Angeli
Tel. 0758043094 - Fax 0758043538

**★★★ DAL MORO ASSISI GALLERY
HOTEL**
Via Santarelli - Fraz. S. Maria Angeli
Tel. 0758043688 - Fax 0758041666

★★★ DAL MORO (Dip.)
Via Santarelli
Fraz. S. Maria Angeli
Tel. 0758043688 - Fax 0758041666

★★★ DEI PRIORI
Corso Mazzini, 15
Tel. 075812237 - Fax 075816804

★★★ FONTEBELLA
Via Fontebella, 25
Tel. 075812883 - Fax 075812941

★★★ FRATE SOLE
Via S. Bernardino da Siena
Fraz. S. Maria Angeli
Tel. 0758043848 - Fax 0758043828

★★★ GIOTTO
Via Fontebella, 41
Tel. 075812209 - Fax 075816479

★★★ HERMITAGE
Via G. degli Aromatari, 1
Tel. 075812764 - Fax 075816691

★★★ IL CASTELLO
Viale Marconi, 1/b
Tel. 075812384 - Fax 075812567

★★★ IL PALAZZO
Via S. Francesco, 8
Tel. 075816841 - Fax 075812370

★★★ LA TERRAZZA
Via F.lli Canonichetti
Tel. 075812368 - Fax 075816142

★★★ LA TORRETTA
Via del Ponte, 1 - Fraz. Petrignano
Tel. 0758038778 - Fax 0758039474

★★★ LE GRAZIE
Via Madonna delle Grazie
Fraz. S. Maria Angeli
Tel. 0758043850 - Fax 0758043851

★★★ LOS ANGELES
Via Los Angeles - Fraz. S. Maria Angeli
Tel. 0758041339 - Fax 0758041225

★★★ PANDA
Via G. Di Vittorio, 5 - Fraz. S. Maria Angeli
Tel. 0758043680 - Fax 0758043681

★★★ PORTA NUOVA
Viale Umberto I, 21
Tel. 075812405 - Fax 075816539

★★★ PORZIUNCOLA
Piazza Garibaldi, 10 - Fraz. S. Maria Angeli
Tel. 0758043677 - Fax 0758042890

★★★ SAN FRANCESCO
Via San Francesco, 48
Tel. 075812281 - Fax 075816237

★★★ SAN PIETRO
Piazza San Pietro, 5
Tel. 075812452 - Fax 075816332

★★★ TERRA NATIA
Via Berlinguer, 5 - Fraz. S. Maria Angeli
Tel. 0758044193 - Fax 0758044193

★★★ UMBRA
Via degli Archi, 6
Tel. 075812240 - Fax 075813653

★★★ VIOLE - Via Assisana, 67
Tel. 0758065409 - Fax 0758064635

★★★ WINDSOR SAVOIA
Viale Marconi, 1
Tel. 075812210 - Fax 075813659

★★ ALEXANDER
Piazza Chiesa Nuova, 6
Tel. 075816190 - Fax 075816190

★★ ANCAJANI
Via Ancajani, 16
Tel. 075815128 - Fax 075815129

★★ ASCESI
Via Frate Elia, 5
Tel. 075812420 - Fax 075812420

★★ BELVEDERE
Via Borgo Aretino, 13
Tel. 075812460 - Fax 075816812

★★ BERTI
Piazza S. Pietro, 24
Tel. 075813466 - Fax 075816870

★★ CENACOLO FRANCESCANO
Via Patrono d'Italia - Fraz. S. Maria Angeli
Tel. 0758041083 - Fax 0758040552

★★ COUNTRY HOUSE
Via di Valecchie, 41
Tel. 075816363 - Fax 075816155

★★ DA ANGELO
S. Rufino Campagna, 35/c
Tel. 075812821 - Fax 075812502

★★ DA RINA
Piaggia S. Pietro, 22
Tel. 075812817 - Fax 075816824

★★ DEL VIAGGIATORE
Via S. Antonio, 14
Tel. 075816297 - Fax 075813051

★★ DOMUS PACIS ASSISI
Piazza Porziuncola - Fraz. S. Maria Angeli
Tel. 0758043530 - Fax 0758040455

★★ EXCELSIOR
Via Tiberio di Assisi, 2/a
Tel. 075812328 - Fax 075813006

★★ GREEN
S. Giovanni Campiglione, 110
Tel. 075813710 - Fax 075812335

★★ IDEALE PER TURISTI
Piazza Matteotti, 1
Tel. 075813570 - Fax 075813020

★★ IL MANIERO
Via S. Pietro Campagna, 32
Tel. 075816379 - Fax 075815147

★★ LA COCCINELLA
Via Gorghi, 3 - Fraz. Rivotorto
Tel. 0758064367 - Fax 0758064367

★★ LA FORTEZZA
Vicolo Fortezza, 19/b
Tel. 075812418 - Fax 0758198035

★★ LA QUIETE
Via S. Pietro Campagna, 95
Tel.075816227 - Fax 075812775

★★ LIETA OASI
Via G. Cipolla, 3 - Fraz. S. Maria Angeli
Tel. 0758041354 - Fax 0758041354

★★ LIETO SOGGIORNO
Via A. Fortini
Tel. 075816191

★★ MINERVA
Piazzetta R. Bonghi, 7
Tel. 075812416 - Fax 075813770

★★MODERNO
Via G. Carducci, 37 - Fraz. S. Maria Angeli
Tel. 0758040410 - Fax 0758040647

★★PALLOTTA
Via S. Rufino, 6
Tel. 075812307 - Fax 075812307

★★POSTA E PANORAMIC
Via S. Paolo, 17
Tel. 075816202 - Fax 075812558

★★PROPERZIO
Via S. Francesco, 38
Tel. 075813188 - Fax 075815201

★★ROMA
Piazza Santa Chiara, 13/15
Tel. 075812390 - Fax 075816743

★★SAN GIACOMO
Via S. Giacomo, 6
Tel. 075816778 - Fax 075816779

★★S. MARIA
Via Lorenzetti, 2 - Fraz. S. Maria Angeli
Tel. 0758041030 - Fax 0758041622

★★SAN RUFINO
Via Porta Perlici, 7
Tel. 075812803 - Fax 075812803

★★SOLE - Corso Mazzini, 35
Tel. 075812373 - Fax 075813706

★★SOLE (Dip.) - Corso Mazzini, 20
Tel. 075812922 - Fax 075813706

★★VILLA ELDA
Via S. Pietro Campagna, 139
Tel. 0758041756 - Fax 0758041501

★★VILLA VERDE
Via Sacro Tugurio, 111 - Fraz. Rivotorto
Tel. 0758065444 - Fax 0758064312

★ANFITEATRO ROMANO
Via Anfiteatro Romano, 4
Tel. 075813025 - Fax 075815110

★BELLAVISTA
Via S. Pietro Campagna, 140
Tel. 0758041636 - Fax 0758042492

★CAVALLUCCI
Via S. Pietro Campagna, 4
Tel. 075813279

★DONNINI
Via Los Angeles, 47
Fraz. S. Maria Angeli
Tel. 0758040260 - Fax 0758040260

★FONTANELLA
Via S. Maria della Spina, 18
Fraz. Rivotorto
Tel. 0758064400 - Fax 0758064182

★FONTEMAGGIO
S. Rufino Campagna, 8
Tel. 075813636 - Fax 0758013749

★GROTTA ANTICA
Via Macelli Vecchi, 1
Tel. 075813467

★IL DUOMO
Vicolo S. Lorenzo, 2
Tel. 075812742 - Fax 075812803

★ITALIA
Vicolo della Fortezza
Tel. 075812625 - Fax 0758043749

★LA ROCCA
Via Porta Perlici, 27
Tel. 075812284 - Fax 075812284

★LA TAVOLA ROTONDA
Via Los Angeles, 9
Fraz. S. Maria degli Angeli
Tel. 0758043328 - Fax 0758043329

★LO SCUDO
Via S. Francesco, 3
Tel. 075813196 - Fax 075813196

★MARCONI
Piazza D. Alighieri, 3
Fraz. S. Maria Angeli
Tel. 0758041156 - Fax 0758041156

★MONTECAVALLO
Via Patrono d'Italia, 46
Fraz. S. Maria Angeli
Tel. 0758040867 - Fax 0758040867

★PATRONO D'ITALIA
Via Patrono d'Italia, 48
Fraz. S. Maria Angeli
Tel. 0758040221 - Fax 0758040867

★PORZIUNCOLA (Dip.)
Via Micarelli, 3 - Fraz. S. Maria Angeli
Tel. 0758043677 - Fax 0758042890

★SAN GIACOMO (Dip.)
Via S. Giacomo, 4
Tel. 075816778 - Fax 075816779

★VICTOR
Via S. Maria della Spina, 18 - Fraz. Rivotorto
Tel. 0758064526 - Fax 0758065562

★VIGNOLA
Via S. Bernardino da Siena, 23
Fraz. S. Maria Angeli
Tel. 0758040652 - Fax 0758040652

★VILLA CHERUBINO
Via Patrono d'Italia, 39
Fraz. S. Maria Angeli
Tel. 0758040805 - Fax 0758040226

Farm Stay Holidays

AGRICOLA NIZZI
Costa di Trex, 65
Tel. 075813378 - Fax 0758043749

BRIGOLANTE
Costa di Trex, 31
Tel. 075802250 - Fax 075802250

CARFAGNA SERGIO
San Pietro Campagna, 144
Tel. 075813742

CASA DEL VENTO
Fraz. Porziano, 84
Tel. 075802150 - Fax 075802150

CASA FAUSTINA
Frazione Mora, 28
Tel. e Fax 0758039377

CASALE 3M
Frazione S. Presto, 92
Tel. 075802178 - Fax 075802178

CASA NUOVA
Pian della Pieve, 55
Tel. 075802143- Fax 075802143

CASA ROSA
Fraz. S. Maria di Lignano
Tel. 075802322 - Fax 075802322

COLCACIONE
Costa di Trex - Tel. 0758019010

GIARDINO FIORITO
Via S. Tecla, 5 - Palazzo di Assisi
Tel. 0758038233

IL CASTELLO
Costa di Trex, 25
Tel. 075813683 - Fax 075813683

IL GIARDINO DEI CILIEGI
Via Massera, 6 - Capodacqua
Tel. 0758064091 - Fax 0758069070

IL GIRASOLE
S. Pietro Campagna, 199
Tel. 075813449 - Fax 075813449

IL GROTTINO
S. Pietro Campagna, 112
Tel. 075816131

IL MANDORLO
Str. Francesca, 6
Tel. 075813555 - Fax 075813555

IL PODERE
Via Casa Madonna, 11 - Petrignano
Tel. 0758038806 - Fax 0758038806

IL QUERCIONE
Via S. Petrignano, 3 - Rivotorto
Tel. 0758065058 - Fax 0758065058

IL SENTIERO
Via delle Acacie, 3 - S. Vitale
Tel. 0758065573 - Fax 0758065573

I TIGLI - IL FRASSINO
Costa di Trex
Tel. 075802410

LA CANTINA
S. Pietro Campagna, 112/B
Tel. 075813386 - Fax 075813386

LA CASTELLANA
Costa di Trex, 4
Tel. 0758019046 - Fax 0758019046

LA MORA
Via Campagna - S. Maria Angeli
Tel. 0758041164 - Fax 0758041164

L'ANTICO MULINO
S. Maria di Lignano - Tel. 075802316

LA PANORAMICA
S. Pietro Campagna
Tel. 075813482 - Fax 075813482

LA PIAGGIA
S. Pietro Campagna, 60
Tel. 075816231 - Fax 0758198469

LA PIEVE
Pieve S. Nicolò, 17
Tel. 0758199018 - Fax 0758199018

LA ROCCA
Rocca S. Angelo
Tel. 0758039082 - Fax 0758039289

TENUTA LE SELVE
Frazione Armenzano
Tel. 0758019003

LE ANTICHE MACINE
S. Pietro Campagna, 112
Tel. 075812263

LE CASACCE
Fraz. Porziano - Tel. 075802217

LE COCCE - Pian della Pieve, 62
Costa di Trex - Tel. 075802152

LE COLOMBE
Rocca S. Angelo, 42/43
Tel. 0758098101 - Fax 0758099336

LE QUERCE
Pian della Pieve
Tel. 075802332 - Fax 0758025000

LOCANDA DELL'ANGELO
Fraz. Mora, 24
Tel. 0758039780

LONGETTI
S. Pietro Campagna, 35
Tel. 075816175 - Fax 0759869562

LO SPERONE
Voc. Reale, 129 - Castelnuovo
Tel. 0758043257 - Fax 0758043257

MALVARINA
Via Malvarina, 32 - Capodacqua
Tel. 0758064280 - Fax 0758064280

MIRANDA
San Presto, 94 - Tel. 075802130

MONTICELLO DI SANT'ALPESTRO
San Presto, 113
Tel. 075802222- Fax 075802222

OASI BATTIFOGLIA
Loc. Paradiso, 33
Tel. 075802320 - Fax 075802320

PODERE LA FORNACE
Frazione Tordibetto
Tel. 0758019537 - Fax 0758019630

SAN MARTINO
S. Pietro Campagna, 80
Tel. 075813563 - Fax 075813563

S. MARIA DELLA SPINA
Rivotorto
Tel. 0759869755 - Fax 0758004346

SASSO ROSSO
Via Renaro, 26 - Capodacqua
Tel. 0758065454 - Fax 0758064861

SIENA
Str. della Pescara, 64 - Tel. 075813382

SILVIA LETIZIA
Costa di Trex, 6/a - Tel. 0758019008

VILLA GABBIANO
Capodacqua
Tel. 0758065278 - Fax 0758065278

Restaurants

RISTORANTE IL GIRASOLE
06081 Assisi (PG) - 67, v. Cannara
Rivotorto d'Assisi
tel. 075 8043281

LA LOCANDA DEL CARDINALE
06081 Assisi (PG) - 8, p. del Vescovado
tel. 075 812206, 075 815243
fax: 075 816691

RISTORANTE PANTAREI
06081 Assisi (PG) - 8, fraz. Petrignano
tel. 075 8038565-075 8039393

RISTORANTE LA COCCINELLA
06081 Assisi (PG) - 3, fr. Rivotorto
Rivotorto d'Assisi
tel. 0742 651594-075 8064204
075 8064367

TRATTORIA DEGLI ANGELI
06081 Assisi (PG) - 47, v. Los Angeles
tel. 075 8043016

RISTORANTE FONTEMAGGIO
06081 Assisi (PG) - 8, v. S. Rufino Campagna
tel. 075 813636 - fax 075 813749

HOTEL SUBASIO
06081 Assisi (PG) - 2, v. Frate Elia
tel. 075 812206 - fax 075 816691

RISTORANTE '75
06081 Assisi (PG) - str. 75 - Loc. Rivotorto
tel. 075 8065194 - 075 8065455

**RISTORANTE PIZZERIA
BELLAVISTA**
06081 Assisi (PG) - 140,
voc. San Pietro Campagna
tel. 075 8041636, 075 8042492
fax. 075 8041636

TRATTORIA DA ELIDE
06081 Assisi (PG) - 48, v. S. Patrono
tel: 075 8043422

RISTORANTE "DA BOCCIONE"
06081 Assisi (PG) - S. Gregorio
tel: 075 8038675, 075 8038438

AI CAVALIERI - LOCANDA
06081 Assisi (PG) - 47, v. Matteotti
Petrignano di Assisi
tel: 075 8030011 - fax: 075 8030011

L'ARALDO
06081 Assisi (PG) - 5, v. Berlinguer
S. Maria degli Angeli
tel: 075 8044193 - fax: 075 8044193

ANFITEATRO ROMANO
06081 Assisi (PG) - Via Teatro Romano
tel: 075 815110

RISTORANTE METASTASIO
06081 Assisi (PG) - Via Metastasio
tel: 075 816525

BRILLI BISTROT GASTRONOMICO
06081 Assisi (PG) - Via Los Angeles
tel: 075 8043433

CHIARA DI PERAZZONE E BELLINA
06081 Assisi (PG) - Via dei Macelli Vecchi
tel: 075 813467

E' PIZZA
06081 Assisi (PG) - Via Portica
tel: 075 813623

GIARO
06081 Assisi (PG) - Via Los Angeles
tel: 075 8043016

GIRARROSTO LA FORTEZZA
06081 Assisi (PG) - Vicolo Fortezza
tel: 075 812993

IL MENESTRELLO
06081 Assisi (PG) - Via S. Gregorio
tel: 075 812334

LE CARAVELLE
06081 Assisi (PG) - Via Los Angeles
tel: 075 8040531

OSTERIA LA PIAZZETTA
06081 Assisi (PG)
Via S. Gabriele dell'Addolorata
tel: 075 815352

OSTERIA POZZO DELLA MENSA
06081 Assisi (PG) - Via Pozzo della Mensa
tel: 075 8155236

PIZZERIA CAMPING
06081 Assisi (PG) - Località Campiglione
tel: 075 813305

RISTORANTE BUCA DI S. FRANCESCO
06081 Assisi (PG) - Via Brizi Eugenio
tel: 075 813780

RISTORANTE CARFAGNA
06081 Assisi (PG) - Voc. S. Pietro Campagna
tel: 075 813063

RISTORANTE DA CECCO
06081 Assisi (PG) - Piazza S. Pietro
tel: 075 812437

RISTORANTE DAL MORO
06081 Assisi (PG) - Via Ponte Grande
tel: 075 812969

RISTORANTE DEGLI ORTI
06081 Assisi (PG) - Via Salita degli Orti
tel: 075 812549

RISTORANTE GIARDINO PARADISO
06081 Assisi (PG) - Via Padre Antonio Giorgi
tel: 075 812843

RISTORANTE IL FRANTOIO
06081 Assisi (PG) - Vicolo Illuminati
tel: 075 812977

RISTORANTE IL FRANTOIO
06081 Assisi (PG) - Via Fontebella
tel: 075 815442

RISTORANTE LA FORTEZZA
06081 Assisi (PG) - Vicolo Fortezza
tel: 075 812418

**RISTORANTE LA LOCANDA
DEL PODESTA'**
06081 Assisi (PG) - Via S. Giacomo
tel: 075 813034

RISTORANTE LA LOCANDA DI GIOTTO
06081 Assisi (PG) - Via Portica
tel: 075 812121

RISTORANTE LA ROCCHICCIOLA
06081 Assisi (PG) - Località Rocca S. Angelo
tel: 075 8038161

RISTORANTE LA STALLA
06081 Assisi (PG) - Via S. Rufino Campagna
tel: 075 812317

RISTORANTE MEDIO EVO
06081 Assisi (PG) - Via Arco dei Priori
tel: 075 813068

RISTORANTE PIZZERIA I MONACI
06081 Assisi (PG) - Piazzetta Verdi
tel: 075 812512

**RISTORANTE PIZZERIA
LA BASILICA**
06081 Assisi (PG) - Via Protomartiri Francescani
tel: 075 8044491

RISTORANTE S. FRANCESCO
06081 Assisi (PG) - Via S. Francesco
tel: 075 812329

**RISTORANTE TAVERNA
DEI CONSOLI**
06081 Assisi (PG) - Vicolo Fortezza
tel: 075 812516

**RISTORANTE TAVERNA DELL'ARCO DA
BINO**
06081 Assisi (PG) - Via S. Gregorio
tel: 075 812383

RISTORO LA ROSA
06081 Assisi (PG) - Via Alcide De Gasperi
tel: 075 8044555

SIROGES
06081 Assisi (PG) - Via Del Torrione
tel: 075 816873

L'ARALDO
06088 Santa Maria Degli Angeli (PG)
VIA DIAZ ARMANDO
tel: 075 8043318

**ALBERGO RISTORANTE
VILLA CHERUBINO**
06088 Santa Maria Degli Angeli (PG)
VIA PATRONO D'ITALIA
tel: 075 8040226

RISTORANTE IL CANTICO
06088 Santa Maria Degli Angeli (PG)
VIA PATRONO D'ITALIA
tel: 075 8044234

RISTORANTE IL CAMINETTO
Via Portica, 29/b - Tel. 075/815126

RISTORANTE LA LANTERNA
VIA S. RUFINO, 41/B - Tel.: 075/813142

PIZZERIA IL DUOMO
Via Porta Perlici - 075/8163276

RISTORANTE DA DIOVANNINO
Loc. Pontegrande - Tel.: 075/813698

RISTORANTE IL PINO
Loc. S. Presto - Tel.: 075/802102

RISTORANTE OSTERIA DI CAMBIO
Via Cambio Palazzo - Tel. 075/8030046

RISTORANTE PAMBIANCO
Viale Michelangelo Palazzo
075/8037102

**RISTORANTE IL CASTELLO
DI PETRIGNANO**
Via del Castello – Petrignano
Tel. 075/8038565

RISTORANTE TRANCANELLI
Via G. Matteotti – Petrignano
Tel. 075/8038044

RISTORANTE CASTEL S. GREGORIO
San Gregorio - Tel. 075/8038009

TRATTORIA SANTUCCI
Via Patrono d'Italia - 075/8042835

**RISTORANTE PIZZERIA LA TAVOLA
ROTONDA**
Via Los Angeles - 075/8043328

Index